P9-DFQ-833

VIRGINIA WOOLF: THE FRAMES OF ART AND LIFE

Virginia Woolf: The Frames of Art and Life

C. RUTH MILLER

Assistant Professor of English
University of Toronto

St. Martin's Press   New York

First published in the United States of America in 1988

Printed in Hong Kong

ISBN 0–312–01914–9

Library of Congress Cataloging-in-Publication Data
Miller, C. Ruth.
Virginia Woolf: the frames of art and life.
Bibliography: p.
Includes index.
1. Woolf, Virginia, 1882–1941—Aesthetics.
I. Title
PR6045.072Z8167   1988   823'.912   88–4440
ISBN 0–312–01914–9

To Lawrence

Contents

Preface

The frame is one of many metaphors and models Virginia Woolf derived from painting, and, judging from critical response, one of the least obtrusive. Still, the frames in her writings and her exploration of the principles of framing reveal the extent to which she anticipated the contemporary interest in the threat that the marginal poses to the integrity of the centre. The frame, which charts the disputed border between life and art, is the archetype of the marginal. Recently, literary theorists have been drawn to the model provided by the frame and have suggested that it does not merely mark but, in fact, defines the difference between life and art. As Stanley Fish has noted, 'literature . . . is language around which we have drawn a frame, a frame that indicates a decision to regard with a particular self-consciousness the resources language has always possessed'.[1]

In Virginia Woolf's writings, the frame is often portrayed as a representative of the ordering powers of art. Framing encourages the selective vision needed to perceive the enclosed scene as a unified work of art, but Virginia Woolf was suspicious of the limitations and distortions that such a process entails. This distrust, evident throughout her writings, prompted R. L. Chambers to describe her works as successful attempts 'to take the frame from the picture'.[2] Yet, as the analysis of her views on art and life in Chapter 1 reveals, Virginia Woolf recognised that frames are necessary, in life as well as art.

The frame typifies the arbitrary conventions required to identify and circumscribe works of art. As a writer, Virginia Woolf was particularly interested in its literary equivalent. Recently, semiologists have examined the way in which extra-literary material such as book covers, title-pages and prefaces perform the role of a frame, but, usually, literary 'framing' refers to the practice of embedding one narrative in another. While Virginia Woolf used this technique – conspicuously in *Between the Acts* – there is evidence that she also conceived of a literary frame that resembled the frame of a painting more directly, one that would create the effect of spatial boundaries. A difficulty she frequently addresses in her diaries is to find a way to 'enclose' (*D2*, p. 13) or 'contain' (*D3*, p. 18) the works she envisaged, a way 'to embody . . . the exact shapes my brain holds' (*D*4, p. 53). In the early stages of *The Waves*, she noted in her diary that she 'was not satisfied . . . with the frame' (*D*3, p. 219). As will be seen in Chapter 2, the principal advantage of the novel, for Virginia Woolf, was the flexibility of its frame.

Virginia Woolf's attitude towards framing provides an insight into her views on art and life and her criteria for comparisons among the arts and genres. Yet critical attention tends to be confined to the frames within her works.[3] Most frequently noted is the framing effect of the window in *To the Lighthouse*.[4] The examination of these frames in Chapter 3, however, reveals that the passing references that are generally made to their effects in studies of Virginia Woolf do not comprehend the various and complex ways in which they serve as both instances and emblems of her theories of art.

In writing this book I have not followed a chronological pattern, but this should not be taken to suggest that Virginia Woolf's theories of art remained unchanged throughout the course of her career. I have deliberately avoided a chronological approach because it almost inevitably results in the developmental fallacy – the often implicit assumption that each work in a writer's canon represents a refinement of its predecessor. Very few would argue that this is true of Virginia Woolf. The structure of this book is circular rather than linear: the third and final chapter provides the specific examples that prompted the theories outlined in Chapters 1 and 2.

I wish, finally, to thank Professors Henry Auster, Susan Dick, Gary Harrington and Michael Millgate for their advice and encouragement. To Professor S. P. Rosenbaum, I am especially indebted for scrupulous guidance. I cannot presume, in a few words, to thank my husband, Lawrence Miller, for the kind of support and assistance that I have grown to depend upon.

Acknowledgements

The extracts from *Between the Acts*, *Mrs Dalloway*, *To the Lighthouse*, and *Collected Essays*, volume 2 by Virginia Woolf, copyright © 1978, 1950, 1941, 1927, 1925 by Harcourt Brace Jovanovich, Inc., renewed 1969, 1955, 1953 by Leonard Woolf, are reprinted by kind permission of the Estate of Virginia Woolf, The Hogarth Press, and Harcourt Brace Jovanovich, Inc.

List of Abbreviations

BA	*Between the Acts*
BP	*Books and Portraits*
D1, D2, D3, D4, D5	*The Diary of Virginia Woolf*, 5 vols
E1, E2, E3, E4	*Collected Essays*, 4 vols
HH	*A Haunted House and Other Short Stories*
JR	*Jacob's Room*
L1, L2, L3, L4, L5, L6	*The Letters of Virginia Woolf*, 6 vols
MB	*Moments of Being*
MD	*Mrs Dalloway*
ND	*Night and Day*
O	*Orlando: A Biography*
RF	*Roger Fry: A Biography*
RO	*A Room of One's Own*
TL	*To the Lighthouse*
VO	*The Voyage Out*
W	*The Waves*
Y	*The Years*

1

Art and Life

The frame of a painting seems to provide an immediate answer to questions concerning the location of the boundary between life and art. Yet such an answer is problematic, since the status of the frame itself remains uncertain; it does not clearly belong to either sphere. The frame first appears as part of a painting, an indication that the perceiver should view its contents as art. From the point of view afforded by the painting itself, however, the frame is an arbitrary convention belonging to the realm of ordinary life. The frame, then, cannot be identified with either life or art; rather, it signals the shift from one to the other.[1] In Virginia Woolf's 'The Lady in the Looking-Glass' and Roger Fry's 'An Essay in Aesthetics', the frame of a mirror is used to suggest the transference of aesthetic criteria to life. That Virginia Woolf would choose to explore the implications of a frame may be seen as a consequence of her association with painters and aestheticians. Although the influence of Roger Fry, in particular, was considerable, Virginia Woolf's theories of art sometimes appear to have developed in opposition to his views.[2] Her acceptance of the metaphors and models that his speculations provided without a corresponding commitment to the theories themselves is evident when one compares their descriptions of the effect of the frame.

In 'An Essay in Aesthetics', Fry remarks upon the difference between a street scene perceived by an individual directly and the same scene when watched in a mirror:

> in the mirror, it is easier to abstract ourselves completely, and look upon the changing scene as a whole. It then, at once, takes on the visionary quality, and we become true spectators, not selecting what we will see, but seeing everything equally, and thereby we come to notice a number of appearances and relations of appearances, which would have escaped our notice before,

owing to that perpetual economizing by selection of what impressions we will assimilate, which in life we perform by unconscious processes. The frame of the mirror, then, does to some extent turn the reflected scene from one that belongs to our actual life into one that belongs to the imaginative life. The frame of the mirror makes its surface into a very rudimentary work of art, since it helps us to attain to the artistic vision.   (*Vision and Design*, p. 25)

In 'A Lady in the Looking-Glass', Virginia Woolf describes letters which have fallen onto a table underneath a looking-glass:

There they lay on the marble-topped table, all dripping with light and colour at first and crude and unabsorbed. And then it was strange to see how they were drawn in and arranged and composed and made part of the picture and granted that stillness and immortality which the looking-glass conferred. They lay there invested with a new reality and significance and with a greater heaviness, too, as if it would have needed a chisel to dislodge them from the table. And, whether it was fancy or not, they seemed to have become not merely a handful of casual letters but to be tablets graven with eternal truth – if one could read them, one would know everything there was to be known about Isabella, yes, and about life, too.   (*HH*, p. 89)

Fry observes that it is the frame of the mirror that enables the transformation from life to an elementary work of art. Virginia Woolf is not so explicit, but it is the frame of the looking-glass that is responsible for ordering and composing the letters. The frame is mentioned twice in the preceding pages of her story: 'One could see a long grass path leading between banks of tall flowers until, slicing off an angle, the gold rim cut it off' (*HH*, p. 86); 'the mistress of the house . . . had gone down the grass path in her thin summer dress, carrying a basket, and had vanished, sliced off by the gilt rim of the looking-glass' (p. 87).

For Fry, the frame confers significance: a 'visionary quality' is granted to an ordinary prospect. It also imposes unity: once enclosed, 'the changing scene' may be perceived 'as a whole'. The frame encourages an aesthetic response in which we 'abstract ourselves completely' and become 'true', democratic spectators, released from our usual dependence upon an unconscious process of selection. Such a vision transposes the spectator from the realm of 'actual life' to that of the 'imaginative life' which, Fry maintains later in the essay, is the 'freer and fuller life' (*Vision and Design*, p. 27). Finally, Fry's conception of framing suggests inclusiveness as well, since we no longer select but see 'everything equally'.

In 'The Lady in the Looking-Glass', the effects that Fry attributes to the mirror's frame are inverted or exaggerated. The letters are granted a greater significance as a consequence of being framed. Virginia Woolf's looking-glass, like Fry's, transposes its contents from one ontological realm to another; the letters are 'invested with a new reality'. But their change in status is oppressive: they acquire 'a greater heaviness, too, as if it would have needed a chisel to dislodge them'. Virginia Woolf projects aspects of the perceiver's response to the letters themselves: enclosed by the mirror, they possess the 'truth' which Fry associates with the spectator who ceases to select. But the 'truth' of the letters is a judgemental, 'eternal truth' which will penetrate and expose not merely the individual but life itself. By framing the letters, the 'crude' is refined, but the process is deathly. At first 'dripping with light and colour', the letters are now 'granted . . . stillness and immortality'. The implication that art requires the renunciation of life tends to subvert our response to Fry's advice to 'abstract ourselves completely'. And, finally, Fry's concept of framing is an inclusive one, but Virginia Woolf's is brutally exclusive: Isabella is 'sliced off' by the frame of the looking-glass.

THE OPPOSITION OF ART AND LIFE

In Fry's essay and Virginia Woolf's short story, the frame is perceived as a representative of the ordering powers of art, whether it is the order that art imposes upon life or design upon vision.[3] The narrator's attitude towards the frame in 'The Lady in the Looking-Glass' is indicative of the suspicion with which Virginia Woolf viewed any such imposition. Virginia Woolf never systematically outlined her aesthetic priorities: the terms of her argument changed continually and the attitudes she held towards the relationship between life and art are so various that it is quite easy to find support for contradictory conclusions. While some maintain that her work is governed by an unprecedented commitment to the representation of life, others see it as the reflection of a belief, considered characteristic of Bloomsbury, in the autonomy of art and the primacy of formal concerns. Her vacillations, however, give a more detailed sense of the balance she hoped to achieve in her writing than any explicit statement of her aims. As she wrote in her diary, 'the more complex a vision . . . the less it is able to sum up & make linear' (*D*4, p. 309). It would be beside the point to scrutinise Virginia Woolf's random comments upon life and art, apart from their context, in an effort to uncover what would necessarily seem a naïve and partially formulated aesthetic. Quite reasonably, she allowed herself a writer's liberty with words and arguments, rather than restricting herself to a philosopher's exactitude. In order to elucidate her views, then, it is necessary to make useful distinctions without avoiding apparent contradictions.

In its most basic form, the relationship between life and art is perceived as an opposition. The claims of life compete with those of art. Yet Virginia Woolf seems to have been equally suspicious of both the elevation of art which she associated with Henry James and the pre-eminence granted to life in E. M. Forster's *Aspects of the Novel*. It is not surprising that, in her chapter 'The Balance of Art and Life: Definition by Disagreement', Jane Novak focuses on Virginia Woolf's contradictory responses to James and Forster. While, in 'The Art of Fiction', Virginia Woolf defended James against Forster's judgement in *Aspects of the Novel*, in her diary, she criticised *The Wings of the Dove* in terms very reminiscent of Forster's:

> His [Henry James's] manipulations become so elaborate towards the end that instead of feeling the artist you merely feel the man who is posing the subject. . . . He becomes merely excessively ingenious . . . . one ceases to have any feeling for the figure behind. Milly thus manipulated, disappears.   (*D*2, p. 136)

It would be misleading, however, to suggest that Virginia Woolf considered Forster a representative of life and James a representative of art. Upon closer examination, it seems that her real quarrel was with James's conception of art and Forster's of life. In the passage quoted above, she argues that when James's manipulations are too elaborate he ceases to be 'the artist'. Reciprocally, in her response to Forster in 'The Art of Fiction', she observes that 'at this point the pertinacious pupil may demand: "What is this 'Life' that keeps on cropping up so mysteriously and so complacently in books about fiction? . . . Surely the definition of life is too arbitrary, and requires to be expanded"' (*E2*, p. 53). Although Virginia Woolf did not attempt to supply more satisfactory definitions, throughout her writings certain qualities are recurrently associated with life and others with art.

'Now is life very solid, or very shifting?' (*D3*, p. 218) is a question which is repeated in different forms throughout Virginia Woolf's novels and diaries. The answer, of course, varies; life has both aspects and each held a particular attraction for Virginia Woolf. The solid quality of life, however, is often sought in her writings and rarely found: 'Why is there not a discovery in life?' she asks in her diary, 'Something one can lay hands on & say "This is it?"' (*D3*, p. 62). At times she seems to suggest that we can only attribute solidity to life by a momentary act of faith or love. It is, the narrator of *Jacob's Room* maintains, one of the 'conditions of our love' that a sudden glimpse of Jacob in his chair is 'of all things in the world the most real, the most solid, the best known to us' (*JR*, p. 116). Paradoxically, the narrator's conviction is, itself, evidence of the tenuousness of her claim, since it is her habit to advance fantastic theories with certainty and 'facts' with extreme tentativeness. To believe that life is not entirely random and transitory may require the faith in God and historical continuity that characterises the deceptively simple statements of Mrs Swithin in *Between the Acts*. For her, the Victorians are 'Only you and me and William dressed differently' (*BA*, p. 203). At times Virginia Woolf herself was impressed by the persistence of certain elements in human nature and conventions, and speculated 'that though we change; one flying after another, so quick so quick, yet we are somehow successive, & continuous – we human beings' (*D3*, p. 218).

Life also seems to gain a sense of solidity through its association with 'reality', 'truth' and 'fact'.[4] These terms are, of course, quite as ambiguous as 'life' itself. Virginia Woolf did, on occasion, reiterate the familiar paradoxes that art creates a 'new' or higher level of reality and that fictive truth is more satisfying than the half-truths of fact. But 'reality', 'truth' and 'fact' also retain more traditional associations in her writings and are considered, if not tangible, uncompromising and empirically verifiable. After the publication of *Jacob's Room*, Virginia Woolf responded rather defensively to Arnold Bennett's criticism that she was unable to create characters that survive: 'I daresay its true, however, that I haven't that "reality" gift. I insubstantise, wilfully to some extent, distrusting reality – its cheapness. But to get further. Have I the power of conveying the true reality?' (D2, p. 248). Although she continued to regard Bennett's conception of reality (which she qualified with quotation marks) as inferior to her own, her several references to his remark in subsequent years suggest that he had, in a sense, voiced her own doubts. Later, in *The Years*, she tried to portray '"real" life' (D4, p. 152) – it is noteworthy that the quotation marks persist after fifteen years – which she also referred to as 'ordinary waking Arnold Bennett life' (D4, p. 161). It may well have been Bennett's comment which prompted her strategy in *Mrs Dalloway*, which followed *Jacob's Room*, to introduce memories and 'dig out beautiful caves behind my characters' (D2, p. 262) when Clarissa was in danger of becoming 'in some way tinselly' (D3, p. 32).

Despite this 'discovery', as she called it in her diary, Virginia Woolf continued to doubt her ability to convey 'real' life, and was particularly impressed by Ethel Smyth's ability to evoke the physical presence of the people she described in her memoirs: 'I like corners to figures: your Brahms one might stub one's toe against' (L5, p. 168). The tangible quality of an aesthetic argument by Roger Fry also impressed her: 'it grazes so many solid objects in its passage that it acquires solidity' (RF, p. 258). It may be that a similar strategy accounts for the preponderance of references to boots and shoes in Virginia Woolf's fiction. They recur as the substantial, if unprepossessing, representatives of 'reality', 'truth' and 'fact'.[5] They are at once reassuring and uncompromising in their ordinariness, persistence and contact with the earth. The banal aspect of life they represent undercuts the unrestrained speculations of Bernard in *The Waves*. Like Virginia Woolf herself, he fears his characterisations are too ephemeral: 'These are fantastic pictures – these are figments, these visions of friends in absence, grotesque, dropsical, vanishing at the first touch of the toe of a real boot' (W, pp. 126–7). This discrepancy recurs with greater poignancy at the end of *Jacob's Room*. In contrast to a fleeting evocation of Jacob by windblown leaves, his pair of old shoes unnecessarily endures. The stern reality represented by boots and shoes also represses our vague, mystical impulses towards union with our fellow men. In *Between the Acts*, Mrs Swithin asks Isa

'Did you feel . . . what he said: we act different parts but are the same?'

'Yes', Isa answered. 'No,' she added. It was Yes, No. Yes, yes, yes, the tide rushed out embracing. No, no, no, it contracted. The old boot appeared on the shingle.   (*BA*, p. 251)

The aspect of life that is characterised by shoes and boots is not always so dispiriting, however. In *To the Lighthouse*, Lily Briscoe manages to evade Mr Ramsay's impossible demands for sympathy when she, quite spontaneously, compliments him on his boots. Although she is immediately ashamed of the incongruity of her response, Lily is reprieved:

Mr Ramsay smiled. His pall, his draperies, his infirmities fell from him. Ah yes, he said, holding his foot up for her to look at, they were first-rate boots. . . . They had reached, she felt, a sunny island where peace dwelt, sanity reigned and the sun for- ever shone, the blessed island of good boots. (*TL*, pp. 237–8)

Yet, as was noted earlier, the 'solid' aspect of life is rarely found in Virginia Woolf's writings. Far more commonly life is perceived as 'shifting' and ephemeral, a 'luminous halo' in her familiar formulation, rather than a substantial boot. Life is the penumbra created by a multitude of simultaneous and continually fluctuating impressions. It is chaotic, uncontainable, and, when it comes into contact with the restrictions imposed by concentration, it is inevitably disruptive: 'I meant to write about death, only life came breaking in as usual' (*D2*, p. 167); 'What happens is, as usual, that I'm going to write about the soul, & life breaks in' (*D2*, p. 234). Yet whenever attention is focused upon life itself, it perversely ceases to 'break in' and 'escapes' instead: 'Indeed most of life escapes, now I come to think of it: the texture of the ordinary day' (*D2*, p. 298). Life is particularly adept at eluding the apparatus of art. In her diary, Virginia Woolf wrote that 'the greatest book in the world' would be one which could 'catch' thoughts 'before they became "works of art"' (*D3*, p. 102). One should not, therefore, criticise Bennett, Galsworthy and Wells too severely for allowing something so characteristically evasive as life to escape. Their offence lies in their complacent acceptance of 'materialism' as a substitute (*E2*, p. 104). There is a certain falsity involved in every effort to draw the disparate elements of life together and make one thing. Virginia Woolf's writings suggest that one must recognise the necessary deception before complying with the demands of

the world. Many of her characters share Clarissa Dalloway's sense
of contraction when 'some call on her to be her self, drew the parts
together, she alone knew how different, how incompatible and
composed so for the world only into one centre, one diamond,
one woman who sat in her drawing-room' (*MD*, p. 57).

It would seem that life in its 'shifting' aspect is often conflated
with the present moment in Virginia Woolf's writing. In her diary,
she closely echoes Mrs Ramsay's 'Life stand still here' (*TL*, p. 249)
with her own 'Time stand still here' (*D4*, p. 102). It is impossible
to capture the present moment or to escape the consciousness of
death. These realisations concentrate and intensify experience. For
Virginia Woolf this transitoriness is itself compelling. It is what
prompted her to endow the newspaper and the post with 'romance'
(*D1*, p. 186). Even the telephone, 'which interrupts the most serious
conversations and cuts short the most weighty observations, has
a romance of its own' (*E2*, p. 157). Throughout Virginia Woolf's
fiction certain characters tend to represent the present moment.
Its transience is reflected by the vacillations and contradictions of
Isa in *Between the Acts*, who is 'the age of the century' (*BA*, p. 26),
and by the fluidity of Jinny in *The Waves*, who realises, even as a
child, that her beauty depends upon the 'here and now'. The
paradigmatic representative of the elusive present is Jacob Flanders.
As a result, he is perhaps the least satisfactorily realised character
in Virginia Woolf's fiction. *Jacob's Room* is not only an elegy to a
young man who must remain shadowy and half-glimpsed, it is
also a homage to all that is ephemeral. Letters are 'Venerable . . .
infinitely brave, forlorn, and lost' (*JR*, p. 150). The traditional
embodiments of transitory beauty are also invoked: 'But real
flowers can never be dispensed with. If they could, human life
would be a different affair altogether. For flowers fade . . .' (p. 135);
'if you talk of a beautiful woman you mean only something flying
fast which for a second uses the eyes, lips, or cheeks of Fanny
Elmer, for example, to glow through' (pp. 188–9).

If life is, at times, synonymous with the present in Virginia
Woolf's writing, art tends to be associated with the past. This
association may be taken to rather absurd lengths. Virginia Woolf
mocks Mrs Hilbery's eulogies for a lost age of great men and great
art in *Night and Day*.[6] The morbid effect of such an atmosphere
upon the living is revealed when Katharine Hilbery compares
Ralph Denham's countenance – which is coloured by 'a deeply
running tide of red blood' (*ND*, p. 9) – unfavourably with the faces

of 'her dead heroes' (p. 10). This attitude is more rigorously parodied in *Orlando*. Nick Green, who shares Orlando's longevity, mourns the passing of famous writers, unconcerned that the contemporaries he castigated in the sixteenth century are the same men he reveres in the nineteenth. Still, the temptation to associate art with the past is difficult to resist. Virginia Woolf often commented upon the difficulty of judging the work of contemporaries:

> the living poets express a feeling that is actually being made and torn out of us at the moment. One does not recognize it in the first place; often for some reason one fears it; one watches it with keenness and compares it jealously and suspiciously with the old feeling that one knew.   (*RO*, p. 22)

In contrast, the books of the past, she observed in an essay, have a 'complete finality' (*E2*, p. 40). The title of the essay, 'Hours in the Library', contains, itself, an implicit comparison of the past and the present, for it is also the title of a collection of literary essays by Leslie Stephen. Virginia Woolf noted in her diary that her contemporaries seemed unable to achieve the 'solid statue that father left – that exists no longer' (*D4*, p. 73).

In a letter to Ethel Smyth, Virginia Woolf wrote 'A masterpiece is I think something said once and for all, stated, finished, so that its there complete in the mind, if only at the back' (*L5*, pp. 143–4). The past is finished as well and, in a sense, dead. One may distance oneself from it, acquire a perspective on it, set it within a context and endow it with unity. In 'Street Haunting', Virginia Woolf compares our present experiences with those of six months ago when we were 'calm, aloof, content' (*E4*, p. 164):

> The sights we see and the sounds we hear now have none of the quality of the past; nor have we any share in the serenity of the person who, six months ago, stood precisely where we stand now. His is the happiness of death; ours the insecurity of life. He has no future; the future is even now invading our peace. It is only when we look at the past and take from it the element of uncertainty that we can enjoy perfect peace.   (*E4*, p. 164)

The effect of the past on our perception of the scene in this passage is similar to the effect of the frame on the narrator's perception of the letters in 'The Lady in the Looking-Glass'. The creation of boundaries, whether temporal or spatial, encourages the observer to compose his impressions into a harmonious whole. Art relies upon such processes of enclosure, selection and ordering. They enable the observer to perceive a work of art as one thing; its relations become necessary, rather than arbitrary. In contrast, life is an 'uncircumscribed spirit' (*E2*, p. 106). Like the present moment, it does not provide a vantage point outside itself which would enable us to determine its perimeters. In 'An Essay in Aesthetics', Roger Fry argues that one of the distinctions between actual life and the imaginative life of art is that, in the former,

> the need for responsive action hurries us along and prevents us from ever realizing fully what the emotion is that we feel, from coordinating it perfectly with other states. In short, the motives we actually experience are too close to us to enable us to feel them clearly. They are in a sense unintelligible. In the imaginative life, on the contrary, we can both feel the emotion and watch it.   (*Vision and Design*, p. 30)

A comparison of Fry's observation with Virginia Woolf's remarks in 'Street Haunting' reveals the same sort of opposition that was evident in their descriptions of the effect of the frame: for Fry, the fruits of reflection are clearly preferable to the 'unintelligible' data of actual life, whereas Virginia Woolf again associates the peace afforded by reflection with death. Even so, she realised that the unity of a work of art provides the reassuring sense of solidity so rarely found in life. Louis, in *The Waves*, who feels threatened by the apparently random and fragmentary nature of experience, takes refuge in the attempt to create 'a steel ring of clear poetry' (*W*, p. 139). His tendency to equate the opposition of art and life with that of order and chaos is a common one. Virginia Woolf herself, in 'The Narrow Bridge of Art', foresees an ideal book in which the author will

> bring to bear upon his tumultuous and contradictory emotions the generalizing and simplifying power of a strict and logical imagination. Tumult is vile; confusion is hateful; everything in a work of art should be mastered and ordered.   (*E2*, p. 228)

Virginia Woolf sometimes maintained that the 'reality' of life is inferior to that of art. The latter requires a more rigorous abandonment of personal interest. In her diary she wondered whether her art conveyed 'the true reality. . . . Or do I write essays about myself?' (*D2*, p. 148). Clive Bell also equates 'the ultimate reality' with 'the thing in itself'.[7] The idea that art is disinterested, an end in itself rather than a means, is, of course, a familiar one, associated primarily with Kant but revived for Bloomsbury by G. E. Moore's *Principia Ethica*. It provides the background for E. M. Forster's statement in *Anonymity: An Enquiry* that 'Information points to something else. A poem points to nothing but itself' (p. 14). The need for anonymity in art and the pernicious effect of any attempt to use art as a platform are themes which recur throughout Virginia Woolf's writings. In *A Room of One's Own*, despite her feminism, she argues that, when writing fiction, 'It is fatal for a woman to lay the least stress on any grievance; to plead even with justice any cause; in any way to speak consciously as a woman' (*RO*, p. 157). This is dramatised in *To the Lighthouse* when Charles Tansley's comment 'Women can't paint, women can't write' (*TL*, p. 78) infects Lily's response to her art. Lily is unable to regain her vision until, 'subduing all her impressions as a woman to something much more general', she becomes 'once more . . . her picture' (p. 86). Tansley's egotism taints his own perception of art, as well. Mrs Ramsay realises that 'that was what his criticism of poor Sir Walter, or perhaps it was Jane Austen, amounted to. "I – I – I"'(p. 165). Mr Ramsay demands reassurance and recognition as well, but he is redeemed by his disinterested response to art: 'Raising the book a little to hide his face he . . . forgot himself completely . . . forgot his own bothers and failures completely' (p. 185).

THE RELATIONSHIPS BETWEEN ART AND LIFE

Although certain qualities may be attributed to life and others to art, Virginia Woolf did not generally separate the two in order to consider their rival claims. More often, a conflict arises from opposing notions of the relationship between life and art. David Lodge, in *The Modes of Modern Writing*, concludes his preliminary survey by dividing the 'attitudes and arguments we have reviewed . . . into two large and opposing groups'.[8] One side holds that 'art imitates life', the other that 'life imitates art'. Although it is necessary to establish two opposing relationships between life and art, it seems that the time-honoured word 'imitates' in Lodge's formulation creates more problems than it solves. One can, for example, maintain that art is finally accountable to life without diminishing its function to mere imitation. Roger Fry commented that the Post-Impressionists sought 'not to imitate life, but to find an equivalent for life' (*Vision and Design*, p. 190). Wilde's inversion, 'life imitates art', certainly does not reflect the way most people are conscious of living, nor does it encompass many other ways in which art determines the quality of life. Perhaps a more comprehensive approach to this conflict of priorities could be taken by opposing the claims that 'art represents life' and 'life is perceived as art'. To suggest that there is an opposition between these two propositions is perhaps misleading, for they are not necessarily mutually exclusive. The real conflicts in Virginia Woolf's aesthetics have been obscured by the failure to make two critical distinctions at this point: for Virginia Woolf, art can represent life in an important way *and* in a trivial way; and life can be perceived as art in an enriching way *and* in a restrictive way.

It was noted earlier that Virginia Woolf criticised the Edwardians' preoccupation with sociological and economic issues as a substitute for the proper task of the novelist – to capture the spirit of life. As a result, the novels of Wells, Bennett and Galsworthy represent life in a trivial way. Similarly, Clive Bell and Roger Fry denounced the Academicians who, by concentrating on mere verisimilitude, neglected the artist's primary challenge – to create 'significant form'. In *Virginia Woolf: The Echoes Enslaved*, Allen McLaurin commends J. K. Johnstone for noting the similarities between Virginia Woolf's opposition to the 'materialism' of the Edwardians and Fry's criticism of photographic representation.[9] These two attacks are analogous but not identical. It is necessary to avoid the tendency to assume, as McLaurin does, that Virginia Woolf was therefore hostile to photographic representation. McLaurin's corollary – that the novels of Wells, Bennett and Galsworthy constitute a literary form of photographic representation – is also misleading. Indeed it could be argued that photography fulfils the aspiration Virginia Woolf often expressed to represent 'the thing itself before its made into anything' (*L3*, p. 321) with less distortion than literature or painting. There is evidence that Virginia Woolf was intrigued by photographs, particularly those taken by her aunt, Julia Margaret Cameron. In collaboration with Roger Fry, she published a collection of Cameron's photographs, and she also succeeded, despite the difficulties involved, in publishing photographs in the first editions of *Orlando, Flush* and *Three Guineas*.[10]

The perceiver of a work of art may also trivialise the way in which art represents life by having an egocentric rather than disinterested response. Virginia Woolf's satirical portrayals of such attitudes are consistent with the Bloomsbury ethos mentioned earlier. Art is no longer an end in itself but the means to self-gratification or higher social status. In this respect, Virginia Woolf shared the views of Clive Bell and Roger Fry; their agreement is emphasised by her tendency to choose paintings as the objects of such inadequate aesthetic attitudes in her fiction. In *Mrs Dalloway*, Sir William Bradshaw's interest in art is, in fact, a means of establishing his reputation as a cultured man, as well as yet another way to coerce his wife: 'But Sir William Bradshaw stopped at the door to look at a picture. He looked in the corner for the engraver's name. His wife looked too. Sir William Bradshaw was so interested in art' (*MD*, p. 291). Sir William's appreciation of a work of art would clearly be hampered by the anonymity advocated by Bloomsbury.

The difference between art that relies upon various personal associations and art that offers disinterested contemplation is often portrayed in Virginia Woolf's novels as the difference between a portrait and a work of art. The portraits of Richard Alardyce in *Night and Day* and the ancestor in *Between the Acts* look at the characters in the novels, and insist that the characters enter into a personal relationship with them. On the other hand, the lady who is a 'picture' in *Between the Acts* is simply looked at as a work of art.[11] The picture of Mrs Pargiter in *The Years* goes through a transformation which reinforces the role of the perceiver in determining the effect of a work of art. At the beginning of the novel, the picture is definitely a portrait which taunts Delia, in particular, with the reminder that her mother is still alive. In the final section of the novel, Peggy realises that the portrait has become a formal, uncommunicative work of art: 'She looked at the picture of her grandmother as if to ask her opinion. But she had assumed the immunity of a work of art; she seemed . . . to be indifferent to our right and wrong' (*Y*, p. 352).

In his discussion of *To the Lighthouse*, Allen McLaurin argues that, considering 'the agreement between Roger Fry and Virginia Woolf in their attack on photographic representation in painting and literature, it follows that a thoughtful artist like Lily Briscoe would not be portrayed as a representational painter'.[12] This statement illustrates the confusion that arises when one fails to recognise the potential for art to represent life in a significant way as well as in a trivial way. As was noted earlier, Virginia Woolf was not necessarily as hostile to photographic representation as McLaurin suggests. A more serious error is that 'photographic representation' becomes merely 'representation' later in the sentence. Given that McLaurin assumes that Fry and Virginia Woolf considered photographic representation to be trivial, it does not follow that they extended the same criticism to all manner of representation. In fact, McLaurin observes in an earlier chapter that Fry had 'a more balanced attitude toward representation than many critics suggest'.[13] Finally, this statement and the argument that follows it classify Lily's painting as non-representational. Yet its distinction lies in its capacity to represent the reality behind appearances. Many critics have observed the resemblance between Lily's purple triangle and the 'wedge–shaped core of darkness' (*TL*, p. 99) that Mrs Ramsay intuits in solitude. (McLaurin himself notes the association of Mrs Ramsay with the colour purple.) Like Miss La Trobe's conception for her next play, which is enacted by Isa and Giles at the end of *Between the Acts*, Lily's painting proves that art is able to penetrate the surface of life to represent its more essential aspects.

Art may also represent life in a significant way by fulfilling life's potentialities. At times, it seems that Virginia Woolf subscribed to the Aristotelian notion that art completes what nature leaves unfinished. She portrays Sir John Paston reading Chaucer and Lydgate because they 'showed him the very skies, fields, and people whom he knew, but rounded and complete' (*E3*, p. 8). Mrs Swithin tells Miss La Trobe 'you've made me feel I could have played . . . Cleopatra', a declaration which the latter interprets as 'You've stirred in me my unacted part' (*BA*, p. 179). As Robert Kiely observes, for Mrs Swithin the pageant is 'a relief from time, an ordered revelation of the possibilities unrealised in a single life'.[14] In this context, the affiliations of art with the past and life with the present are replaced by more traditional correlations: life is perceived as the realm of time while art escapes time's limitations. The role of the artist, then, is redemptive. Virginia Woolf imagines herself 'a deliverer advancing with lights across the waste of years' (*E4*, p. 120) when, in her essays, she rescues the lives of little-known diarists and correspondents from the obscurity of the past. This crusade may also be expressed in terms of order and chaos. The artist, in this context, resembles the God of creation. In *The Waves*, Bernard's 'daily battle' is to retrieve the world 'from formlessness with words' (*W*, p. 295).

As mentioned earlier, the priorities in the relationship of life and art may be reversed – life may be perceived as art. This kind of perception may be restrictive, as John Maynard Keynes observed in a memoir:

> I fancy we used in old days to get round the rich variety of experience by expanding illegitimately the field of aesthetic appreciation . . . classifying as aesthetic experience what is really human experience and somehow sterilizing it by this mis-classification.[15]

Keynes is referring to his student years at Cambridge and the combined influence of the Apostles and G. E. Moore's *Principia Ethica*. If Cambridge was responsible for such extended aesthet-icism, it also fostered the sensitivity Keynes exhibits to the dangers of neglecting human experience in favour of art. The type of aestheticism that Keynes describes is condemned in the novels and essays of E. M. Forster, who was himself an Apostle. And, although Forster maintained that Virginia Woolf was fortunate to have escaped 'the Palace of Art',[16] she too criticised the tendency to distance oneself from a human situation by treating it as a work of art. The repercussions of such behaviour are illustrated by the theatrical metaphors in *Mrs Dalloway*. By treating the war like a show, Septimus sins against human nature. The moment of intimacy between Peter and Clarissa comes only after she stops ob-serving his visit as if it were 'five acts of a play that had been very exciting and moving' (*MD*, p. 72), and walks over to the window to join him. In a more sinister form, Sir William Bradshaw's 'proportion' may be seen as the consequence of imposing the ordering devices of art – selection, exclusion and pattern – upon life:

> Worshipping proportion, Sir William not only prospered himself but made England prosper, secluded her lunatics, forbade

childbirth, penalised despair, made it impossible for the unfit to propagate their views until they, too, shared his sense of proportion.   (*MD*, pp. 150–1)

This intolerance of the vagaries of human nature is represented, in a less extreme form, by Neville in *The Waves*, Bonamy in *Jacob's Room* and Edward Pargiter in *The Years*. The sterility of their common objective, 'to addict oneself to perfection' (*W*, p. 94), is emphasised by their latent or practised homosexuality and by their devotion to the impersonal clarity of the ancient Greeks. Virginia Woolf's short story, 'Solid Objects', is an undisguised allegory of the consequences of such behaviour. The protagonist's obsessive search for a perfectly shaped object culminates in his discovery of a fragment of meteorite. Its black, cold presence in his room signals that he is finally impervious to any human appeal. In *The Voyage Out*, a similar effect is created by the 'views'. From the expanded perspective they afford, man appears quite insignificant. Although Clarissa Dalloway is parodied in *The Voyage Out*, she is, perhaps unwittingly, perceptive enough to distrust the views: '"Honestly, though", said Clarissa, having looked, "I don't like views. They're too inhuman"' (*VO*, p. 63).

Certain techniques of art may be used to diminish the complexity of life. One of Rachel Vinrace's early methods of dealing with other people is to transform them into symbols. As a result, 'these odd men and women' become 'featureless but dignified, symbols of age, of youth, of motherhood, of learning, and beautiful often as people upon the stage are beautiful' (*VO*, p. 35). Virginia Woolf herself, while she tried to refine her perception in order to concentrate upon the thing in itself, recognised that the impulse towards symbols and metaphors is difficult to resist. Rhoda at the string quartet is frustrated by the opacity of her analogies: '"Like" and "like" and "like" – but what is the thing that lies beneath the semblance of the thing?' (*W*, p. 176). Often these comparisons which obscure reality are derived from the hackneyed phrases of mediocre literature. Elizabeth Dalloway is oppressed by such clichés: 'People were beginning to compare her to poplar trees, early dawn, hyacinths, fawns, running water, and garden lilies; and it made her life a burden to her' (*MD*, p. 203). In such a case, life is restricted and distorted when it is perceived as a work of art.

Often the effect is reversed – life is enriched when it is perceived as art. Certainly the 'artists in life' in Virginia Woolf's fiction enhance life with their combinations and creations. Mrs Ramsay and Clarissa Dalloway have received particular attention in this context. It could easily be argued that Mrs Ramsay's 'triumphs' gratify her vanity or that Clarissa Dalloway's parties disguise her inability to love. But these reservations are, in turn, qualified by several factors. First, Mrs Ramsay and Clarissa are often judged on the evidence provided by their own self-scrutiny. It is Mrs Ramsay herself who wonders if 'all this desire of hers to give, to help, was vanity' (*TL*, p. 68). Clarissa is quite aware of the accusation Peter intends when he calls her the perfect hostess: '(she had cried over it in her bedroom), she had the makings of the perfect hostess, he said' (*MD*, p. 13). Also, the characters within the novels who view the successes of Clarissa and Mrs Ramsay with scepticism are finally compelled to admire them. The malicious satisfaction Lily Briscoe takes in the failure of Mrs Ramsay's matchmaking is far outweighed by the 'revelation' she owes to Mrs Ramsay: 'Mrs Ramsay saying "Life stand still here"; Mrs Ramsay making of the moment something permanent . . . this was of the nature of a revelation' (*TL*, p. 249). Augustus Carmichael's disapproval of Mrs Ramsay is presented obliquely and may be the product of her own perception, although he certainly seems to be exempt from the general devotion to her. Yet his homage to Mrs Ramsay after the dinner party suggests that he admires her sterner qualities. He appreciates the work of art that she has managed to create and, by opening the door for her, seems to be helping her to accept its transience: 'Without knowing why, she felt that he liked her better than he had ever done before; and with a feeling of relief and gratitude she returned his bow and passed through the door which he held open for her' (*TL*, p. 172). Although, as a young man, Peter Walsh resented Clarissa's social manner, which he realised was somehow related to her refusal to marry him, he still 'admired her courage; her social instinct; he admired her power of carrying things through' (*MD*, p. 94). When he returns to England, posing as world-weary and indifferent, he finds himself nevertheless on the way to Clarissa's party 'with the belief upon him, that he was about to have an experience' (*MD*, p. 245).

The integrity of Clarissa and Mrs Ramsay as artists is reinforced by their ability to lose their sense of self and become anonymous. This is the quality that Virginia Woolf considered the most difficult for the artist to achieve, yet essential to the creation of works of art. Walking through London, Peter Walsh's perception of the bell of St Margaret's is affected by his thoughts of Clarissa, and he thinks that its sound resembles 'the voice of the hostess . . . reluctant to inflict its individuality' (*MD*, p. 76). Mrs Ramsay can also submerge her individuality 'until she became the thing she looked at – that light for example' (*TL*, p. 101), just as, earlier, Lily became 'once more . . . her picture' (*TL*, p. 86) in order to create. The speculations that Mrs Ramsay enters into as the lighthouse beam traverses her window seem to be characteristic of the artist, since she senses that Lily and Augustus Carmichael share them: 'And to everybody there was always this sense of unlimited resources, she supposed; one after another, she, Lily, Augustus Carmichael, must feel, our apparitions, the things you know us by, are simply childish' (*TL*, pp. 99–100).

THE RECONCILIATION OF ART AND LIFE

To take a further step and consider the novel that represents life that is perceived as art may suggest a way of resolving the conflict of priorities between life and art. Two triadic reconciliations are possible. The first, noted above, is a work of art which represents life perceived as art. There are moments of such perception in all of Virginia Woolf's novels. In *Between the Acts*, particularly, Virginia Woolf focuses on the drama enacted outside the conventional boundaries of art. Indeed, the novel suggests that this triad continues to proliferate until life and art are so confused that, during the pageant, a member of the audience comments on the odd names given to 'real people' (*BA*, p. 149). The second reconciliation occurs when life perceived as art is, in turn, associated with a more comprehensive understanding of life. When Roger Fry observes the street scene in the mirror, he provides an example of life perceived as art. When he goes on to maintain that this type of perception (that is, the imaginative vision associated with art as opposed to the selective vision of ordinary life) is the avenue to a 'freer and fuller life' (*Vision and Design*, p. 27), he creates the second triad. Virginia Woolf also observed that the view of life afforded by art is more satisfactory than that which our ordinary perception provides. In 'The New Biography', she wrote 'it would seem that the life which is increasingly real to us is the fictitious life; it dwells in the personality rather than in the act. Each of us is more Hamlet, Prince of Denmark, than he is John Smith of the Corn Exchange' (*E4*, p. 234).

   Both of these possible reconciliations are based on the positive ways in which art can represent life and life can be peceived as art. There are also counterparts to these triads based on the negative corollaries. In 'Solid Objects', Virginia Woolf introduces John in an impersonal manner and from such a remote perspective that it distances the reader from him, just as John detaches himself from the rest of humanity in his quest for the perfect object: 'The only thing that moved upon the vast semicircle of the beach was one small black spot' (*HH*, p. 79). Art, in this case, represents life that is perceived as art in a restrictive way.[17] It was observed that the frame in 'The Lady in the Looking-Glass' imposed its own order on the objects that the looking-glass reflected. Yet the narrator maintains at the end of the story that the looking-glass reveals the 'truth' about Isabella, even if that truth is that 'there was nothing. Isabella was perfectly empty. She had no thoughts' (*HH*, p. 92). Again a superior understanding of life is invoked. In 'The Lady in the Looking-Glass', Virginia Woolf portrays life perceived as art which, even when it is reductive, reveals the essential aspect of life. For Virginia Woolf, the bleakness of such a revelation is mitigated by the courage one summons to withstand it. In her diary, she describes her descent into her 'great lake of melancholy': 'I feel that if I sink further I shall reach the truth. That is the only mitigation; a kind of nobility. Solemnity. I shall make myself face the fact that there is nothing – nothing for any of us' (*D3*, p. 235).

   In different contexts, several critics have remarked upon Virginia Woolf's attraction to tripartite structures.[18] Yet it seems arbitrary to limit the series of possible interrelations of art and life to three. Depending upon one's perspective, the sequence may continue. 'The Lady in the Looking-Glass', for example, is a work of art representing the triad outlined above. To chart each step in each series, however, would be needlessly exacting. It would also distort one of the principal effects of the interrelations – to reveal the inevitable confusion and interpenetration of life and art. Yet the sense of various levels of remove that such series entail suggests a Platonic conception of art. This is heightened by Virginia Woolf's interest in copies or 'reflections', in 'The Lady in the Looking-Glass' quite explicitly, and elsewhere in her writings as well. In 'A Sketch of the Past', she outlines a possible reconciliation of life and art which is, in fact, a modification of Platonic theory. Where Plato had posited the forms behind the world of appearance, Virginia Woolf substitutes the work of art (merely the copy of a copy in the Platonic formulation). Describing her shock-receiving capacity, she comments

> it is not, as I thought as a child, simply a blow from an enemy hidden behind the cotton wool of daily life; it is or will become a revelation of some order; it is a token of some real thing behind appearances; and I make it real by putting it into words. It is only by putting it into words that I make it whole; this wholeness means that it has lost its power to hurt me. . . . From this I reach what I might call a philosophy; at any rate it is a constant idea of mine; that behind the cotton wool is hidden a pattern; that we – I mean all human beings – are connected with this; that the whole world is a work of art; that we are parts of a work of art. (*MB*, p. 72)

This passage may not be as logically consistent as a rigorous philosopher would wish, and Virginia Woolf is tentative in describing it as 'what I might call a philosophy' and as an 'intuition of mine' (*MB*, p. 72). But it cannot be dismissed as an impulsive notion. Virginia Woolf insists that 'one is living all the time in relation to certain background rods or conceptions. Mine is that there is a pattern hid behind the cotton wool. And this conception affects me every day' (*MB*, p. 73). In a similar manner, Clive Bell's 'fancies' outlined in 'The Metaphysical Hypothesis' chapter of *Art* provide the basis for his further theorising. And though he argues that each reader 'must decide for himself'[19] whether to accept his metaphysical hypothesis or not, it is this hypothesis that accounts for the significance of significant form. Like Virginia Woolf's speculations in 'A Sketch of the Past', Clive Bell's metaphysical hypothesis is Platonic. His indebtedness to Plato, suggested by his choice of the term 'form', is confirmed when he proposes that the artist feels 'something behind' the beauty apparent in the external world (or 'material beauty' in Bell's formulation) in the same way as 'we feel something behind the forms of a work of art'.[20] The closest he comes to describing the 'something' apprehended by the artist is as 'that which lies behind the appearance of all things – that which gives to all things their individual significance, the thing in itself, the ultimate reality'.[21]

It seems that Virginia Woolf and Clive Bell endow the artist with a privileged insight. The reality behind appearance is revealed to him and he, in turn, may communicate his vision in a work of art. But Bell admits that 'All of us, I imagine, do, from time to time, get a vision of material objects as pure forms . . . and at such moments it seems possible, and even probable, that we see them with the eye of an artist'.[22] And Virginia Woolf demystifies the artist's vision even further by placing it within a psychological context. She represents art as a way of explaining the mystery and allaying the pain of a 'sudden violent shock' (*MB*, p. 71): 'It is only by putting it into words that I make it whole; this wholeness means that it has lost its power to hurt me' (*MB*, p. 72). The notion that art is conceived as a means of coping with potentially traumatic situations recurs in the holograph of *The Pargiters*: 'Probably people who have been bullied when they are young, find ways of protecting themselves. Is that the origin of art . . . "making yourself immune by an image"'.[23] In his biography of Virginia Woolf, Quentin Bell also stresses the therapeutic nature of her art: 'Virginia's instinctive response to suffering was always to write'.[24]

In 'A Sketch of the Past', Virginia Woolf supposes that 'the shock-receiving capacity is what makes me a writer' (*MB*, p. 72). Yet, in her novels, she does not confine the glimpses of the pattern behind the cotton wool to artists. During the party in the final chapter of *The Years*, Eleanor Pargiter also wonders if there is 'a pattern; a theme, recurring, like music; half remembered, half foreseen? . . . a gigantic pattern, momentarily perceptible' (*Y*, p. 398). And this speculation is immediately followed by the question 'who makes it?' The same question hovers over the dispersing audience after the pageant in *Between the Acts*: 'He said she meant we all act. Yes, but whose play? Ah, that's the question' (*BA*, p. 233). In 'A Sketch of the Past', having posited the work of art behind the cotton wool, Virginia Woolf immediately and emphatically denies the existence of its creator. Instead, 'we are the words; we are the music; we are the thing itself' (*MB*, p. 72). Without this denial, one might conclude that Virginia Woolf would finally place the claims of art above those of life – the world acts in accordance with the design of a universal work of art. Yet one of the corollaries of her denial of a creator is that the hidden work of art cannot assert its supremacy over life, since it exists only by virtue of our presence as both its material and its perceivers. Life *is* the hidden work of art, not merely the material manipulated by the creator of a work of art, and there can be no conflict of priorities where there is identity. The hidden work of art is 'created' only in so far as we perceive it.

TO SEE LIFE STEADILY AND SEE IT WHOLE

The idea of creation as perception recurs in Virginia Woolf's writings – evidence again of the pervasive influence of G. E. Moore. In 'A Defence of Common Sense' and elsewhere in his philsophy, Moore focuses on the relationship between perception and existence. The effect of his inquiry upon the Cambridge Apostles is described by E. M. Forster at the opening of *The Longest Journey*:

> 'The cow is there,' said Ansell, lighting a match and holding it out over the carpet. . . .
> It was philosophy. They were discussing the existence of objects. Do they exist only when there is some one to look at them? Or have they a real existence of their own? It is all very interesting, but at the same time it is difficult. Hence the cow.[25]

Virginia Woolf was certainly acquainted with this sort of debate and her novels display a familiarity with the perennial formulations of the problem. In *The Years*, for example, Maggie asks 'Would there be trees if we didn't see them?' (*Y*, p. 150). It is a critical commonplace that Leslie Stephen inspired the portrait of Mr Ramsay in *To the Lighthouse*. Indeed, 'father's character, sitting in a boat, reciting We perished, each alone, while he crushes a dying mackerel' was the 'centre' of Virginia Woolf's conception of the novel (*D*3, pp. 18–19). Yet, as S. P. Rosenbaum has noted, Mr Ramsay's philosophical speculations are those of G. E. Moore.[26] As Andrew Ramsay explains to Lily Briscoe, his father writes about 'Subject and object and the nature of reality' (*TL*, p. 40).

Virginia Woolf responded to the commonsense philosophy of G. E. Moore in much the same way as she did to the aesthetics of Clive Bell and Roger Fry. She found the framework of Moore's inquiry more suggestive than its actual propositions. Moore concluded that, although it was not susceptible to irrefutable proof, common sense compelled him to maintain that a material object would remain when he ceased to perceive it. But Virginia Woolf was intrigued by the way in which perception could be considered creative. Although she would not have claimed that the existence of something as substantial as a table depends upon a perceiver, she was very aware of the extent to which the existence of intangibles, such as a sense of identity or a personality, are the products of perception. It is, of course, part of a novelist's profession to 'create characters'. Yet, for Virginia Woolf, Jane Austen and Tolstoy create characters and even worlds of greater dimension than Charlotte Brontë because their characters 'live and are complex by means of their effect upon many different people who serve to mirror them in the round' (*E1*, p. 186). One might argue that this is an aesthetic judgement rather than an ontological claim. Certainly the existence of fictional characters, if they can be said to exist at all, is dependent in a way that the existence of living persons is not. But when Bernard, turning his thoughts to Neville, says 'Let me then create you. (You have done as much for me)' (*W*, p. 91), all manner of existence seems to be regarded as precarious and dependent. Virginia Woolf frequently echoes this thought: in a letter to Molly MacCarthy, she asks 'Yet how do we exist, save on the lips of our friends?' (*L6*, p. 337).

Virginia Woolf generally identified creative perception with sight. In *Jacob's Room*, the narrator suggests that 'the manner of our seeing' is synonymous with 'the conditions of our love' (*JR*, p. 116). Those who are unseen, like Rhoda in *The Waves*, who has 'no face' (*W*, p. 45), are threatened with negation. One of the ways in which Bernard registers the change that follows his loss of self is that he 'saw but was not seen' (*W*, p. 314). The sense of annihilation that is created in the 'Time Passes' section of *To the Lighthouse* is due to the strategy Virginia Woolf mentions in her diary, to make the passage 'all eyeless & featureless' (*D3*, p. 76), which would forbid any effort towards reciprocal identification. Conversely, to share a vision is the closest approximation to immortality possible in life. The characters in *The Waves* 'come together . . . to make one thing, not enduring – for what endures? – but seen by many eyes simultaneously' (*W*, p. 137). Yet, whenever a person is seen by someone else, he becomes aware of the restrictions imposed by the other's preconceptions. The narrator of 'An Unwritten Novel' remarks 'The eyes of others [are] our prisons; their thoughts our cages' (*HH*, p. 20). This notion recurs in *The Waves*. The characters realise that it is necessary to be seen in order to establish their identities, but the process diminishes them. As Neville observes,

'Something now leaves me; something goes from me to meet that figure who is coming. . . . As he approaches I become not myself but Neville mixed with somebody' (*W*, p. 89). This is why Lily Briscoe feels she needs at least fifty sets of eyes in order to see Mrs Ramsay. It accounts for the inclusion of a multiplicity of eyes in Virginia Woolf's novels as well. In *The Waves*, the characters' eyes are associated with various natural images. In *To the Lighthouse*, Mr Ramsay is far-sighted and Mrs Ramsay, short-sighted – a detail which reflects the difference in their natures.

Lily Briscoe has slanted 'Chinese eyes' which may be related to the image of the diagonal line uniting Mr and Mrs Ramsay. Harvena Richter notes that the lines in Lily Briscoe's painting run 'up and across' (*TL*, p. 319) and speculates that these 'slanting lines which finally connect the two masses . . . in Lily's canvas are the enduring emotion between wife and husband which Lily at first did not perceive, seeing them as two different and antagonistic worlds'.[27] In *A Room of One's Own*, as well, the 'union of man and woman' (*RO*, p. 147) is represented by a diagonal line:

> it was like a signal falling, a signal pointing to a force in things which one had overlooked. . . . Now it was bringing from one side of the street to the other diagonally a girl in patent leather boots, and then a young man in a maroon overcoat; it was also bringing a taxi-cab; and it brought all three together at a point directly beneath my window . . . when I saw the couple get into the taxi-cab the mind felt as if, after being divided, it had come together again in a natural fusion.   (*RO*, pp. 144–7)

The role of the diagonal line in Virginia Woolf's writings may have been suggested by Roger Fry's elucidation of paintings. She attended many of his lectures from 1920 (if not earlier) until his death, and in her biography of Fry, she re-creates his technique: 'His long wand, trembling like the antenna of some miraculously sensitive insect, settled upon some "rhythmical phrase", some sequence; some diagonal' (*RF*, p. 262). Again, in her diary, she describes 'Roger rather cadaverous in a white waistcoat. A vast sheet. Pictures passing. . . . Elucidates unravels with fascinating ease & subtlety this quality and that: investigates (with his stick) opposing diagonals'. (*D4*, p. 76). When Lily Briscoe's attention is fully occupied by the painting which will combine the qualities of

Mr and Mrs Ramsay, she encourages her diagonal vision by 'screwing up' (*TL*, p. 243) her eyes.

The eyes of the other artist visiting the Ramsays, Augustus Carmichael, are singular as well: 'like a cat's they seemed to reflect the branches moving or the clouds passing, but to give no inkling of any inner thoughts or emotion whatsoever' (*TL*, p. 21). The eyes are those of an artist who has freed his response from self-interest and reached the state of anonymity desired by Virginia Woolf herself. The indirect presentation of Augustus Carmichael in the novel, almost entirely through the perception of others, reinforces the sense of his self-effacement. By refusing to impose his individuality, he heightens the self-consciousness of other characters. In his presence, Mrs Ramsay questions her motives and Lily feels her efforts are justified. Carmichael's reflecting eyes may be compared to the eyes of the mystic in 'Time Passes' who projects his own aspirations onto his surroundings. A more immediate comparison, however, is made between the vision of the mystic and that of Mrs McNab. While the mystic sees his desire reflected in a mirror provided by nature, Mrs McNab hazards only a 'sidelong leer' (*TL*, p. 203) in the Ramsays' looking-glass, for 'her eyes fell on nothing directly, but with a sidelong glance that deprecated the scorn and anger of the world – she was witless, she knew it' (*TL*, p. 202). Mrs McNab will continue 'to drink and gossip as before' (*TL*, p. 204), whether the mystic celebrates his communion with nature or realises that the war has destroyed his Utopian visions. Survival, particularly after the war, consists in accepting the mixed and fragmentary, not in pursuing absolutes. Mrs McNab's indirect glance is preferable to the mystic's fixed gaze, for it does not seek to fathom mysteries, but respects them.[28]

Still, there is evidence that Virginia Woolf shared with E. M. Forster a nostalgia for the Arnoldian belief in the potential to 'see life steadily and see it whole'.[29] In *Howards End* and his earlier novels, Forster suggests that there is still a chance for the moderns to attain such a vision, but Virginia Woolf felt that the war and the tendency towards specialisation had narrowed the scope of human perception or set it at an odd angle. In 'On Not Knowing Greek', she maintains that 'In the vast catastrophe of the European war our emotions had to be broken up for us, and put at an angle from us, before we could allow ourselves to feel them in poetry or fiction' (*E1*, p. 10). The divisiveness caused by various angles of vision is reminiscent of Babel; in an essay, 'The Leaning Tower',

Virginia Woolf uses the image of a collapsing tower as a metaphor for the effects of war. The movement towards specialisation also emphasises differences rather than similarities. In 'Walter Sickert', Virginia Woolf maintains that specialisation 'accounts for the starved condition of criticism in our time, and the attenuated and partial manner in which it deals with its subject' (*E2*, p. 242). One is reminded again of Forster when, in her diary, she comments 'that is another argument against the specialist. Cant connect' (*D4*, p. 228).

For Virginia Woolf, the prelapsarian ability to see life steadily and see it whole existed in the early days of civilisation and exists again in childhood. The ancient Greeks were able 'to look directly and largely rather than minutely and aslant' (*E1*, p. 10). In 'A Sketch of the Past', she describes a childhood vision of wholeness that she experienced in the garden at St Ives:

> I was looking at the flower bed by the front door; 'That is whole', I said. I was looking at a plant with a spread of leaves; and it seemed suddenly plain that the flower itself was a part of the earth; that a ring enclosed what was the flower; and that was the real flower; part earth; part flower. (*MB*, p. 71).

A similar episode occurs in *Between the Acts* when George, 'grouting in the grass' (*BA*, p. 16), uncovers the roots of a flower: 'the grass, the flower and the tree were entire. Down on his knees grubbing he held the flower complete' (p. 17). But his vision is disrupted when his grandfather Bartholomew surprises him. The terror and frustration George experiences illustrate the effects of an adult's intrusion into a child's Edenic world. But the confrontation is more complex. To a rationalist like Bartholomew, George's vision of unity constitutes an affront to reason. He finds the kind of continuity that is assumed by his sister, Lucy, disturbingly mystical as well. Bartholomew, like Mr Ramsay, shares the philosophical views of G. E. Moore. In *Principia Ethica*, Moore wrote that 'To search for "unity" and "system," at the expense of truth, is not, I take it, the proper business of philosophy, however universally it may have been the practice of philosophers'.[30] But Virginia Woolf empathises with the deflation that George Oliver and James Ramsay experience when their visions are checked by rationalists. There is, throughout her diaries, the sense of a quest for a vision of unity comparable to the one she had as a child in St Ives:

Yet I have some restless searcher in me. Why is there not a discovery in life? Something one can lay hands on & say 'This is it?' . . . It is not exactly beauty that I mean. It is that the thing is in itself enough: satisfactory; achieved.   (*D3*, p. 62)

Despite this desire, she shared Moore's disapproval of unified systems that are the products of wish-fulfilment pursued at the expense of truth. In her writings, the instigators of such systems are mocked. There is an element of self-parody in these portrayals as well, due to her own preoccupation with unity. In an essay, 'The Cosmos', the complacent understanding of Mr Cobden-Sickert is presented with mild irony: 'there was a unity of the whole in which the virtues and even the vices of mankind were caught up and put to their proper uses. Once attain to that vision, and all things fell into their places' (*E4*, p. 94). In *The Voyage Out*, Richard Dalloway's self-serving ideas are more rigorously parodied. 'Conceive the world as a whole' (*VO*, p. 72), he counsels Rachel, but the whole he describes is a machine which revolves around himself. As well as elevating his stature, Dalloway's 'unity' ensures that he need not become personally involved in the misfortunes of others. Rachel finds it 'impossible to combine the image of a lean black widow . . . longing for someone to talk to, with the image of a vast machine' (*VO*, p. 72). The unity Richard Dalloway conceives justifies his sexism as well: the sexes, he argues, complement each other – men fight while women retain their illusions.

As Virginia Woolf was conscious of the possibilities of such self-deception, it is not surprising that she was wary of 'one-making' (*BA*, p. 204). In *The Years*, North remarks that comedy and contrast are the 'only form of continuity' (*Y*, p. 372). The artists Virginia Woolf portrays are, as a result, divided people striving to achieve synthesis. In *Between the Acts*, clichés reinforce this impression: William Dodge belongs to the 'half-breeds' (*BA*, p. 61); Miss La Trobe is not 'altogether a lady' (p. 72); Mrs Swithin has a 'divided glance' (p. 14). Yet, as was noted earlier, Virginia Woolf generally associated art with unity: her artists, therefore, must achieve, if only momentarily, a unified vision. If an artist wishes to communicate a glimpse of the work of art hidden behind the cotton wool of everyday existence, he must attain what Roger Fry called an 'all-embracing vision' (*Vision and Design*, p. 49) as well. The specialist may see one thing, but Virginia Woolf dismissed his limited and exclusive achievement; unity must be inclusive – the hidden work of art contains 'the whole world' (*MB*, p. 72). In 'Phases of Fiction', she praises Proust's ability 'not to enforce a view but to enclose a world' (*E2*, p. 83). Even her childhood vision in the garden at St Ives was inclusive – a flower is not an isolated object as we are encouraged to perceive it but 'part earth; part flower' (*MB*, p. 71). Thus Rhoda in *The Waves* searches for a circle that will 'embrace the entire world' (*W*, p. 244). And, in her diary, Virginia Woolf remarks 'what a discovery that would be – a system that did not shut out' (*D4*, p. 127).

Such a system could only exist when individuals recognise and accept their community with all human beings. In Virginia Woolf's writings, speculations concerning the creator of the hidden work of art are generally followed by another question which, despite various formulations, remains essentially 'Are we one, or are we separate' (*Y*, p. 150). Virginia Woolf was tempted to answer 'one', but she was not prepared to accept a form of mysticism uncritically in order to justify her belief in the desirability of such a communion. In *Mrs Dalloway*, Clarissa's 'transcendental theory' is filtered through the doubtful perspective of Peter Walsh:

> She waved her hand, going up Shaftesbury Avenue. She was all that. So that to know her, or any one, one must seek out the people who completed them; even the places. . . . It ended in a transcendental theory which, with her horror of death, allowed her to believe, or say that she believed (for all her scepticism), that since our apparitions, the part of us which appears, are so momentary compared with the other, the unseen part of us, which spreads wide, the unseen might survive, be recovered somehow attached to this person or that, or even haunting certain places, after death. Perhaps – perhaps.   (*MD*, p. 230)

Clarissa's 'theory' is seen as a product of her 'horror of death', but it is not the product of a naïve understanding – it exists 'for all her scepticism'. And there is evidence in Virginia Woolf's diary that the thoughts she attributed to Clarissa are not very different from her own. But, given a communal conception of life, Clarissa infers that we live after death in other people, while Virginia Woolf tended to stress the bleaker corollary – that part of us dies when another dies. When Goldsworthy Lowes Dickinson died, she felt 'how much of a piece with our friends, like him, we are; it is thus we die, when they die' (*D4*, p. 120). And, again, when she read of Stella Benson's death, she experienced

> A curious feeling . . . that one's response is diminished. Here & Now [an early title for *The Years*] wont be lit up by her: its life lessened. My effusion – what I send out – less porous and radiant – as if the thinking stuff were a web that were fertilized only by other peoples (her that is) thinking it too: now lacks life. (*D4*, p. 193)

These thoughts upon the deaths of friends are presented as momentary revelations. Adults in the twentieth century are not predisposed to see themselves as fragments of a universal whole. The realisation that 'One brain is only a teaspoon or a thimble; and we ought to combine' (*L6*, p. 242) must be encouraged, for it is no longer instinctive. Virginia Woolf herself and the artists she creates in her novels are constantly trying to reconcile apparent disparities or to blur the edges that divide things from one another. In *To the Lighthouse*, Mrs Ramsay's shawl and cloak are images of the envelopment she desires. Her dislike of divisive lines leads her to toss her shawl 'over the edge of the frame' – an incident which is recalled as she 'smoothed out what had been harsh in her manner' with James (*TL*, p. 51). James Naremore observes that Virginia Woolf's attraction to 'watery metaphors' was prompted by her desire 'to overcome boundaries, insisting upon an ideal unity in life'.[31] This is illustrated in *Between the Acts*: the image of the tide which 'rushed out embracing' encourages Isa to agree that 'we act different parts but are the same' (*BA*, p. 251). References to water in Virginia Woolf's writings are not confined to waves and the sea, although these are generally the focus of critical attention. In *The Years*, it is 'the gentle rain' which, oblivious to the distinctions observed by society, 'poured equally over the mitred and the bareheaded' (*Y*, p. 50). Even the differences between human beings and other living creatures threaten to collapse: the characters in *Between the Acts* and *The Years* mimic and are, in turn, mimicked by animals and birds. B. H. Fussell maintains that Virginia Woolf's practice of yoking disparate elements in *Between the Acts* is a 'rhyming' device, a strategy that is parodied by Isa's rhymes which similarly link 'the emotional with the banal, the grandiose with the trivial'.[32] Puns have the same effect, particularly when they are incongruously placed. For example, Mr Bankes, talking to Mrs Ramsay on the telephone, envisages her 'at the end of the line, Greek, blue-eyed, straight-nosed' (*TL*, p. 50). 'Line' conjoins the telephone wire with a tradition of classical beauty. As the above observations suggest, Virginia Woolf's search for an all-embracing vision emerges in a variety of contexts. The deaths which occur in almost every chapter of *The Years* suggest a unification of time as well. Memories of the dead continue to influence the living, and the reader, like the characters, is not allowed to separate the past from the present or the future.

The desire to assimilate also informed Virginia Woolf's various attempts to create some sort of communal medium of expression, a chorus or an anonymous voice. Harvena Richter has noted some varieties of the collective voice and the 'Tiersias' voice in her fiction.[33] In the final section of *The Years*, Virginia Woolf tried to convey the sense of a chorus: 'I am thinking all the time of what is to end Here & Now [an early title]. I want a Chorus, a general statement' (*D4*, p. 236). A 'general' voice is established in *The Waves* by the lack of differentiation in tone or vocabulary among the six characters and by the uniformity imposed by the continual repetition of 'said'.

At first, Virginia Woolf's emphasis on combination is difficult to reconcile with her insistence upon the contemplation of 'the thing in itself'. Indeed, the way in which she brings together disparate objects seems symptomatic of the 'English disease' that she parodies in *Orlando*:

> The malady is too well known. . . . She climbed the mountains; roamed the valleys; sat on the banks of the streams. She likened the hills to ramparts. . . . Trees were withered hags, and sheep were grey boulders. Everything, in fact, was something else.   (*O*, p. 131)

Roger Fry also criticised the English temperament for preferring 'the associations of things' to 'things in themselves' (*RF*, p. 164). Like the metaphors which plague Elizabeth Dalloway, such substitutions threaten the integrity of their referents. But, for Virginia Woolf, the notion that 'everything is something else' had a quite different application as well. As if to draw attention to this difference, the expression is repeated with only a slight variation in another context in *Orlando*. In the final pages of the novel, Orlando sees into that part of the mind 'in which everything is reflected – and, indeed, some say that all our most violent passions, and art and religion, are the reflections which we see in the dark hollow at the back of the head'. Immediately her path became 'partly the Serpentine . . . the sheep were partly tall Mayfair houses; everything was partly something else' (*O*, p. 290). This is the effect that Virginia Woolf sought to create: combination which respects the thing in itself, rather than substitution which dismisses it.

THE NECESSITY OF FRAMES

In 'An Essay in Aesthetics', Roger Fry describes unity in painting as a balance of attractions so that 'the eye rests willingly within the bounds of the picture' (*Vision and Design*, p. 34). For Virginia Woolf, frames establish this balance by exclusion. As a result, her artists are often portrayed forcing boundaries to widen by introducing awkward elements which, at first, appear to ruin the design. Rachel Vinrace's hypothetical widow cannot be assimilated by Richard Dalloway's 'machine' and therefore reveals its inadequacy. Mrs Swithin's late arrival at the pageant, like many of her unpredictable actions, is superficially annoying but fundamentally salutary. Hers is the first in a series of disruptions by the audience. Although Miss La Trobe curses 'the torture of these interruptions' (*BA*, p. 97), they do, in fact, further her efforts to dissolve the barrier between 'art' and 'life'.

When one considers Virginia Woolf's desire for anonymity in art and her conception of inclusive unity, it is not surprising that the artists in her fiction must resist imposing their own design. Clarissa Dalloway, who refuses to stress her individuality, accepts, and even celebrates, the fact that the woman in the opposite house can move outside her field of vision: 'that's the miracle, that's the mystery . . . here was one room; there another' (*MD*, pp. 192–3). To appreciate the 'miracle' and the 'mystery', one must acknowledge the existence of other people and forces beyond the personal sphere. The artist must be 'released from the cramp and confinement of personality' (*E2*, p. 159). For Virginia Woolf, Jane Austen's achievement lay in her ability to set her 'little grain of experience

. . . outside herself' (*E2*, p. 159). And, conversely, she criticised James Joyce for centring his work upon a self which 'never embraces or creates what is outside itself and beyond' (*E2*, p. 108).

One way of liberating a work of art from the tyranny of the artist is to stress the obligation of the audience to assist in its creation. In *Between the Acts*, Virginia Woolf emphasises the extent of the audience's contribution. Even before the pageant begins, Bartholomew remarks 'Our part . . . is to be the audience. And a very important part too' (*BA*, p. 73). The opening and closing lines of the pageant are merely conventions. It does not begin until the audience relaxes its guard: 'Muscles loosened; ice cracked. The stout lady in the middle began to beat time with her hand. . . . The play had begun' (pp. 96–7).[34] Nor does it end until the audience shifts its attention to other matters: 'The play was over, the strangers gone, and they were alone. . . . Still the play hung in the sky of the mind. . . . In another moment it would be beneath the horizon, gone to join the other plays' (pp. 248–9). The collaboration of the artist and the perceiver in the creation of a work of art is not confined to drama. Novels, too, should be 'the healthy offspring of a close and equal alliance' between the reader and the author (*E1*, p. 336). Virginia Woolf's choice of the epistolary form in, for example, 'A Letter to a Young Poet', 'Middlebrow' and *Three Guineas* is further evidence of her conviction that writing is a shared activity. 'Without someone warm and breathing on the other side of the page', she maintains in *Three Guineas*, 'letters are worthless' (p. 8). The collaborative creation of a letter encouraged her sense of the communal nature of existence. In an essay on the correspondence of Walpole and Cole, she observes that 'The only way to read letters is to read them thus stereoscopically. Horace is partly Cole; Cole is partly Horace' (*E3*, p. 111).

There is the suggestion in Virginia Woolf's fiction that if the artist accepts and respects the inherent mystery of what is 'outside' and 'beyond', he is rewarded by those ungovernable forces themselves. Since Miss La Trobe's pageant accommodates and even encourages interruptions, potentially disruptive events come to her aid.[35] Twice the illusion falters; twice Miss La Trobe murmurs 'This is death' (*BA*, pp. 165, 210). But, on the first occasion, 'as the illusion petered out, the cows took up the burden . . . annihilated the gap; bridged the distance; filled the emptiness and continued the emotion' (pp. 165–6). And later, a 'sudden and universal' (p. 210) shower of rain carries the audience across the other perilous gap. Clarissa Dalloway despairs at the beginning of her party: 'She did think it mattered, her party, and it made her feel quite sick to know that it was all going wrong, all falling flat. Anything, any explosion, any horror was better than people wandering aimlessly' (*MD*, p. 253). But suddenly a gust of wind ruffles the curtains, the narrative shifts from Clarissa's thoughts to Ellie Henderson's, and the tone lightens. Another breeze blows out the curtain and the point of view returns to Clarissa who 'saw Ralph Lyon beat it back, and go on talking. So it wasn't a failure after all! it was going to be all right now – her party' (*MD*, p. 256). As Lucio Ruotolo observes, it is, 'mysteriously, as if the space outside somehow affects the moment'.[36] The sense of the wind's divine intervention is heightened by the accompanying 'flight of wings' of the 'birds of Paradise' depicted on the curtain (*MD*, p. 253).

Although the artist should distrust the exclusivity of his designs and the artifice of beginnings and endings, a work of art requires at least a rudimentary framework. In *The Years*, Virginia Woolf tried to dispense with boundaries. Viewed in this light, the novel, which is often considered a return to traditional techniques, becomes one of her more experimental works. The pattern Eleanor Pargiter intuits at the party corresponds to a shape which emerges earlier in the novel and elsewhere in Virginia Woolf's *oeuvre* – in *Night and Day* and an early typescript of *The Voyage Out*.[37] It is a circle surrounded by radiating lines. In *Night and Day*, it could be considered part of the pattern of astronomical imagery because of its likeness to a star. It also prefigures other geometrical shapes in Virginia Woolf's fiction that are intuited when articulation can go no further, like the 'wedge-shaped core of darkness' (*TL*, p. 99) that represents Mrs Ramsay, or the square placed upon the oblong that Rhoda perceives during the string quartet. Only in *The Years*, however, does the circle surrounded by radiating lines become a structural principle. It is a shape that seems to dispense with boundaries, to radiate infinitely. The novel resembles Eleanor Pargiter's summation of her life: 'scene obliterated scene' (*Y*, p. 395). Various characters are introduced and dominate the story for a time, only to be succeeded by others. Their misunderstandings are rarely righted; their intuitions remain unconfirmed. Without a framework in which to set things in relation to each other, it becomes difficult to have a sense of even temporary wholeness. And, as the final scene of *The Years* indicates, the pattern radiates into the inaccessible. The couple Eleanor is watching from the window step into a house, close the door and continue their lives beyond the range of her perception. The reader, straining to come momentarily to rest, is left still drifting outwards. Joan Bennett has argued that *The Years* 'is not wholly successful . . . even after several readings, it does not give the reader the sense of a single, organized whole'.[38] Although such an impression may not have been one of her objectives, Virginia Woolf was, herself, disappointed by the novel's failure to convey her 'whole meaning . . . because it was too big for me to encircle' (*L6*, p. 122). When, in her next novel, Miss La Trobe tries to dispense with conventions by substituting 'ten mins. of present time' (*BA*, p. 209), Virginia Woolf portrays the audience desperately consulting its programmes and concentrating its attention on the 'tick, tick, tick' of the gramophone. As Allen McLaurin observes, 'a frame, that minimum requirement for art, is lacking'.[39]

A frame establishes the boundaries of a painting. Other art forms require other conventions to perform an analogous function. As Clive Bell remarks in *Art*, 'The man who sets out with the whole world before him is unlikely to get anywhere. In that fact lies the explanation of the absolute necessity for artistic conventions'.[40] 'Convention' is, however, a problematic term. J. K. Johnstone, in his discussion of the Bloomsbury group, considers it necessary to distinguish between manners and convention: manners should be cultivated, but convention 'disregards the individual' and is 'often dishonest'.[41] Yet there is no reason for 'convention' to become a term of disparagement, particularly since Virginia Woolf herself did not necessarily consider it one. The confusion arises from the fact that 'convention' is used in two ways which, though not mutually exclusive, have different emphases. One sense of 'convention' is an inherited, often restrictive, custom. As Virginia Woolf remarks in 'Mr Bennett and Mrs Brown', there are resemblances between this sort of convention in life and its counterpart in art: the trivialities of the Victorian drawing-room are paralleled by the inflexible 'two and thirty chapters' of the Edwardian novelists. David Lodge observes that although, at first, it seems that Virginia Woolf's censure is confined to the content of these novels, 'it soon becomes evident that the form, the fictional technique, which Bennett, Wells and Galsworthy are using condemns them to the trivial and transitory content'.[42] Virginia Woolf uses metaphors of imprisonment to describe the effect of these conventions on both her life and her art. Having liberated herself in both spheres (although aware of a temptation to be smooth and politic in her essays), she mocks these conventions in her fiction and non-fiction. In terms of literary theory, one might assume that she would have agreed with the opinion of such critics as Walter Reed and Ian Watt that the novelist's 'attention to any pre-established formal conventions can only endanger his success'.[43]

Yet towards the same understanding of 'convention' Virginia Woolf occasionally expressed another attitude. After a tea with the Sutton Adult School, she wrote in her diary 'the same queer brew of human fellowship, is brewed; & people look the same . . . & come to these odd superficial agreements, wh. if you think of them persisting & wide spread – in jungles, storms, birth & death – are not superficial; but rather profound' (*D3*, p. 22). And in 'A Sketch of the Past', she observes that even the

> Victorian game of manners . . . has its beauty, for it is founded upon restraint, sympathy, unselfishness – all civilised qualities . . . this surface manner allows one to say a great many things which would be inaudible if one marched straight up and spoke out. (*MB*, p. 129)

The conventions of parties and table talk are relied upon continually by the artists of life in Virginia Woolf's novels. It is sometimes comforting to reflect, as Peter Walsh does, that one can depend upon certain established formulae that the 'art of living' (*MD*, p. 84) provides. There is also a counterpart in literary theory to this more positive aspect of conventions in the position, generally associated with T. S. Eliot, that the literary tradition provides the necessary background against which innovation is conceived.

The second sense of 'convention' is simply an agreement. It becomes possible, therefore, to speak of 'new conventions' as Virginia Woolf does in 'Mr Bennett and Mrs Brown'. In artistic terms, convention in this sense provides the framework that the artist offers and the audience accepts in order for a work of art to be communicated. It was noted that, according to David Lodge, Virginia Woolf felt that the form of the Edwardian novel condemned the novelist to trivial subject matter. An inversion of this principle seems to be true of the moderns. The elusive penumbra of impressions that constitutes the proper subject matter of the novel, 'life itself', requires a strict framework in order to make it accessible to the reader. Joan Bennett maintains that Virginia Woolf 'had to invent conventions as rigid or more rigid than the old ones she discards'[44] in order to communicate her vision. In the same way that Lily Briscoe sought a 'framework of steel' to convey her 'butterfly's wing' (*TL*, p. 78), novelists like Virginia Woolf and James Joyce were highly conscious of the structure of their novels and occasionally confined themselves to the Aristotelian unities.

Although this kind of structure may initially appear to be at odds with the portrayal of the random and fleeting impressions of life, a novel which restricts itself to one day is, in fact, merely reflecting a framework that already exists. A day of life imposes its own beginnings and endings, and, to a diarist particularly, days are often seen as self-enclosed entities. It has become a commonplace that we use the conventions associated with art to order and enrich our experience of life. Virginia Woolf was certainly aware of this tendency. In the introduction to *The Common Reader*, she envisages the mind endlessly constructing temporary scaffolds to accommodate its various impressions. She draws attention to its imitation of the ordering and unifying strategies of art in 'The Lady in the Looking-Glass'. The order that the frame imposes on the letters closely resembles the effect of the narrator's 'logical process' which 'set to work on them and began ordering and arranging them and bringing them into the fold of common experience' (*HH*, p. 88).[45] Conversely, the lack of an imposed or perceived design encourages a relaxation of the mind's activity. The party at lunch in *Between the Acts*, mesmerised by an endless view, finds itself drifting to sleep: 'How tempting, how very tempting, to let the view triumph; to reflect its ripple; to let their own minds ripple; to let outlines elongate and pitch over – so – with a sudden jerk' (*BA*, p. 82).

In 'A Sketch of the Past', Virginia Woolf associates her 'moments of being' with particular scenes. Her memories are enclosed by a 'circle of the scene' which is, in turn, 'all surrounded by a vast space' (*MB*, p. 79).[46] This strategy was not determined by aesthetic considerations alone; Virginia Woolf suggests that her 'scene making' is also a psychological necessity: 'These scenes, by the way, are not altogether a literary device – a means of summing up and making innumerable details visible in one concrete picture. . . . But, whatever the reason may be, I find that scene making is my natural way of marking the past' (*MB*, p. 122). Her awareness of the framing effect of such scenes is evident in a diary entry, written when she felt her friendship with Vita Sackville-West had come to an end: 'Well, its like cutting off a picture: there she hangs, in the fishmongers at Sevenoaks, all pink jersey & pearls; & thats an end of it' (*D4*, p. 287). Although it may seem, in 'A Sketch of the Past', that Virginia Woolf considered scene making her own peculiarity, elsewhere in her writings she suggests that it is part of the human condition. The characters in *The Years* envisage each other in typical postures – Sara sitting with a smudge on her nose, or Morris pausing by the lamp post. In an essay entitled 'Three Pictures', Virginia Woolf maintained

> It is impossible that one should not see pictures; because if my father was a blacksmith and yours was a peer of the realm, we must needs be pictures to each other. We cannot possibly break out of the frame of the picture by speaking natural words. (*E4*, p. 151)

Frames are not only required to organise external impressions; they establish a sense of identity as well. Rhoda and Louis suffer from the lack of an 'end in view', even though such an end would be an artificial boundary. In *Mrs Dalloway*, Virginia Woolf tried to convey 'the world seen by the sane & the insane side by side' (*D2*, p. 207). She remarks, in the introduction to the Modern Library edition, that Septimus 'is intended to be her [Clarissa's] double' (p. vi). Virginia Woolf uses this strategy to demonstrate that the bonds which unite Septimus and Clarissa are much stronger than the differences denoted by society's labels 'sane' and 'insane'. One difference which Virginia Woolf does stress, however, is that Clarissa, unlike Septimus, retains the ability to establish the perimeters of her identity. Throughout the novel, diamonds and other images of compression and contraction are associated with Clarissa. Despite the distortion it entails, she is able to become 'one centre, one diamond, one woman who sat in her drawing-room' (*MD*, p. 57). Septimus, on the other hand, is associated with images of melting and diffusion: 'His body was macerated until only the nerve fibres were left. It was spread like a veil upon a rock' (p. 104).[47] In *To the Lighthouse*, Virginia Woolf associates questions with diffusion and sentences with contraction. At the opening of the section 'The Lighthouse', Lily feels that she

> had no attachment here . . . no relations with it, anything might happen, and whatever did . . . was a question, as if the link that

usually bound things together had been cut, and they floated
up here, down there, off, anyhow. How aimless it was, how
chaotic, how unreal.   (*TL*, p. 227)

The final section of the novel can be seen as Lily's attempt to put
the fragments together, 'write them out in some sentence, then
she would have got at the truth of things' (*TL*, p. 228).

With the image of the circle in *The Waves*, Virginia Woolf again
reveals the need for boundaries in life and the dangers that exist
both within and outside of these boundaries.[48] Protective circles of
expectations are provided by society and forged by individuals.
Rhoda and Louis never cease to suffer from a sense of exclusion.
[Louis's chilblains are another 'penalty of an imperfect circulation'
(*W*, p. 226).] Virginia Woolf publicly proclaimed herself an outsider
in *Three Guineas* and privately reflected on the effects of this status
in her diaries: 'people secrete an envelope which connects them &
protects them from others, like myself, who am outside the
envelope, foreign bodies' (*D3*, pp. 12–13). Yet those who are
securely placed within a circle eventually find themselves en-
trapped by it. Even Susan's circle, which is not chosen arbitrarily
but in accordance with the cycle of nature, becomes oppressive
and numbing. More limited circles, like the one Neville creates
with each of his lovers, are like the 'tight iron hoops' associated
with the egotistical young man in the final chapter of *The Years* (*Y*,
p. 389). Gradually the fiction wears thin, and it is revealed that
the circle revolves around a centre which is empty. A need or
deficiency had created a vacuum which had to be filled. In *Mrs
Dalloway*, this is expressed by the 'emptiness' Clarissa discerns
'about the heart of life' (*MD*, p. 48). Clarissa avoided the radical
commitment demanded by Peter Walsh, choosing instead the
stability and independence that marriage with Richard Dalloway
would provide. Thus she lost an inner intensity and direction that
would have determined her identity, but she gained a more diffuse
awareness of things outside herself. She seeks to fill the vacuum
created by her choice with her parties where she becomes, in her
aptly named drawing-room, 'a meeting-point, a radiancy no doubt
in some dull lives, a refuge for the lonely to come to, perhaps'
(*MD*, pp. 57–8).

Clarissa's parties, like works of art, are the product of her desire
'to combine' and 'to create' (*MD*, p. 184). Like an artist, she
succeeds because she is, essentially, detached and impersonal.

Reciprocally, the accusation of insincerity and unreality implicit in the label 'the perfect hostess' may be levelled at artists as well. The exposure of the central emptiness is often accompanied by a disgust with the lies and compromises that underlie art and the fictive structures we impose on life.[49] Frank Lentricchia, in his examination of the implications of Kermode's argument in *The Sense of an Ending*, summarises the basic dilemma:

> Against these values of 'fiction' stand the qualities of 'reality':
> disorder, chaos, a discordant temporality without beginning or
> end, and a world of praxis where ideas always embody the
> consequences of repressive ideology. Yet no sooner is this
> neoidealist, fictive act of consciousness privileged as an act of
> freedom from the determining forces of reality, than it is quickly
> deprivileged by an existentialist investment which sees fictive
> arrangements of being as impoverished in the face of being
> itself. Fictions become lies, fantasies, pregiven paradigms whose
> imposition upon experience constitutes a massive act of 'bad
> faith'.[50]

The 'emptiness about the heart of life' is connected with death. The expression itself reminds the reader of Clarissa's heart trouble. Septimus's suicide creates another absent centre: 'Oh! thought Clarissa, in the middle of my party, here's death' (*MD*, p. 276). When Lily Briscoe perceives the gap that is created by Mrs Ramsay's death, the scene before her 'became like curves and arabesques flourishing round a centre of complete emptiness' (*TL*, p. 275). Yet if the fact of death makes life seem insignificant, it is also what gives life meaning. In her diary, Virginia Woolf links 'the splendour of this undertaking – life' with 'being capable of dying' (*D4*, p. 120). An 'emptier' concept than death is that of 'non-being' which Virginia Woolf describes in 'A Sketch of the Past' as the 'nondescript cotton wool' of daily life (*MB*, p. 70). Yet even 'non-being' provides the background against which 'moments of being' are conceived. Virginia Woolf recognised its value. She remarks that she tried, but failed, to create 'both sorts of being' in *Night and Day* and *The Years* (*MB*, p. 70). Thus, the 'nothingness' or 'emptiness' at the centre of life and art has another aspect that is better described as 'silence' or 'space'. It is the 'zone of silence in the middle of every art' (*E2*, p. 236) that inspires creation and provides the significant contrast. Percival, the absent presence in *The Waves*, is often cited as an embodiment of the significant contrast. The effect is also created by the pause, apparently orchestrated by Mr Ramsay, in the middle of the voyage to the lighthouse: when at last the wind picks up, James's 'relief was extraordinary. . . . But his father did not rouse himself. He only raised his right hand mysteriously high in the air, and let it fall upon his knee again as if he were conducting some secret symphony' (*TL*, p. 288). In *Jacob's Room*, the 'violet-black dab' (*JR*, p. 9) (foreshadowing Jacob's death) which the artist, Steele, strikes on his canvas functions in the same way: 'it was just *that* note which brought the rest together' (p. 10).

It would seem that Virginia Woolf envisaged art and life as a series of compromises. The necessity of frames must be weighed against the distortion they entail. The creation of works of art depends upon the artist's sense of isolation, even emptiness. But there are two aspects of compromise as well. It may appear to be a lie or a mockery, but it can also be seen as a rarely achieved synthesis. In *To the Lighthouse*, these two attitudes towards compromise are explored and the triumph far outweighs the mockery. In the Ramsay's marriage, each supplies what the other lacks. Moreover, Mrs Ramsay herself embodies the spirit of compromise. She is well aware of its humiliating aspects. Yet the reader senses that her apparently trivial acts – covering a ram's skull with a shawl or substituting 'It's going to be wet tomorrow' (*TL*, p. 191) for 'I love you' – represent a reconciliation of the seen and the unseen, the spoken and the unspoken.

2
Towards a Defence of the Novel

To suggest that Virginia Woolf's writings constitute a defence of the novel seems to disregard her rejection of the title 'novelist' (L6, p. 365)[1] and her attempts to rename her works: 'I have an idea that I will invent a new name for my books to supplant "novel"', she wrote in her diary, 'A new ____ by Virginia Woolf. But what? Elegy?' (D3, p. 34). Her own substitutions are often combinations – 'play-poem' (D3, p. 139), 'biographical fantasy' (D4, p. 180), 'Essay-Novel' (D4, p. 129), 'a poet-prose book' (D5, p. 276) – which reveal her reluctance to confine herself to one genre. Still, it was not for reasons of convenience alone that she continued to refer to herself as a novelist and her works as novels. The instances of her dissatisfaction with these terms are far outnumbered by the occasions on which she explores the novel's potential and envisages its development. In fact, one of the primary reasons for her attraction to the novel is that it lends itself to such a variety of names.

The necessity of boundaries in life and art must be admitted, but the perils associated with framing remain – exclusivity, distortion and imposition. The artist is still required to break useless moulds, include the disparate and search for a circle that will enclose all. Virginia Woolf's defence consisted, primarily, in demonstrating that of all the arts and literary genres the novel has the most flexible frame, one that is capable of widening, crumbling and exposing its own limitations. To adapt this frame to her vision was a challenge she set herself as early as 1908: 'I shall re-form the novel and capture multitudes of things at present fugitive, enclose the whole, and shape infinite strange shapes' (L1, p. 356).

The defence of the novel can be seen as an elaboration of a more general case that Virginia Woolf makes for all literature. (Of course, interpreting her scattered observations as a defence, particularly one of that operates on two levels, involves marshalling the

unsystematic and stating the implicit.) The two oppositions examined in this chapter – between literature and the other arts and
between the novel and other genres – are, in many respects,
analogous to the opposition of life and art discussed in Chapter 1.
For Virginia Woolf, the first element in each of these oppositions
represents the complex, the divided, the impure and the chaotic;
therein lies both its offence and its justification.

Virginia Woolf never questioned her early decision to be a writer.
Her remark in a letter to Violet Dickinson in 1904 – 'Pictures are
easier to understand than subtle literature, so I think I shall became
an artist to the public, and keep my writing to myself' (*L1*, p. 170) –
serves more to emphasise the complexities of writing than to
announce a change of allegiance. She also confined herself to
prose. S. P. Rosenbaum has observed that, unlike almost all of the
contemporary novelists of equal stature, she never attempted
poetry, with the exception of the verses she wrote for *Between the
Acts*.[2] Nevertheless, she was drawn to measure her choice against
the background provided by the other arts and genres, primarily
because her circle was composed of their practitioners. Virginia
Woolf's defence of the novel can be seen as a form of self-defence.
It also reveals her allegiance to England and its traditions –
paradoxically, perhaps, since the novel was also her means of
rebellion from that inheritance.

From childhood, Virginia Woolf's future presented itself as a
choice among the arts: according to Quentin Bell, it was determined
in the nursery at Hyde Park Gate 'that Vanessa was to be a painter
and Virginia a writer'.[3] It was a choice that reflected their natures.
'You *are* a painter', Virginia wrote to Vanessa, 'This explains your
simplicity' (*L1*, p. 475). Her essays reveal the extent to which
literature corresponded to her own personality: in 'Phases of
Fiction', 'How Should One Read a Book?' and 'Reading', she
portrays each genre as satisfying a particular mood. The close
relation between her art and her identity is illustrated as well by
the number of occasions in her diaries when, in comparing herself
to Vanessa, she also compared their two *métiers*. Later, as her
acquaintance with writers and painters increased, the basis of
her comparisons broadened. Remembering evenings spent with
Virginia Woolf and her visitors, Gerald Brenan observes that 'the
same themes always came up . . . the difference between the
painter and the writer'.[4] The comparative framework of these
discussions lent itself more readily to isolating the particular
qualities of each art than to formulating a comprehensive theory

of the arts. (Roger Fry often announced his intention to attempt such a formulation, but he never fulfilled it.) In her critical works, Virginia Woolf's perspective is usually that of the writer rather than the artist.

Virginia Woolf's choice of profession was certainly more traditional than her sister's. Although she would belong to a circle in which 'art' was virtually synonymous with 'painting', literature was the only art discussed at Hyde Park Gate, and, for the most part, in the rest of England as well. In her biography of Roger Fry, Virginia Woolf notes his tendency 'to deplore the extraordinary indifference of the English to the visual arts' (*RF*, p. 52). As Allen McLaurin observes,[5] Bartholomew Oliver in *Between the Acts* expresses Fry's sentiments in a conversation with William Dodge: 'Since you're interested in pictures . . . why, tell me, are we, as a race, so incurious, irresponsive and insensitive . . . to that noble art, whereas, Mrs Manresa . . . has her Shakespeare by heart?' (*BA*, p. 67). Yet Virginia Woolf does not suggest that England's preoccupation with its literary tradition is misplaced (indeed, Bartholomew's remark is succeeded by a pageant celebrating it).

By identifying herself with literature, then, Virginia Woolf also identified herself with England (just as, it could be argued, by choosing painting, Vanessa shifted her allegiance to France). *Between the Acts* portrays the early days of England, its literature and Virginia Woolf herself (as her childhood experience is transferred to George Oliver). All three preserve an Edenic innocence. The evocation of an original garden world in *Between the Acts* could be seen as evidence that the novel had its genesis as early as 1931, when Virginia Woolf attended a gala performance in London: 'I got the feeling of this traditional English life; its garden like quality; flowers all in beds and rows; & the ceremony that has been in being so many years. Between the acts we all stood in the street' (*D4*, p. 31). And, as Virginia Woolf saw her own youth reflected in England's, she also connected her later traumas with the upheavals in her country. To Gerald Brenan she wrote 'Every ten years brings, I suppose, one of those private orientations which match the vast one which is, to my mind, general now in the race' (*L2*, p. 598). That this remark occurs in a letter in which she addresses the reasons for the failure of contemporary literature reinforces the sense that Virginia Woolf felt her fate was closely tied to that of England and its writing.

While Virginia challenged Hyde Park Gate on its own terms Vanessa awakened the visual sense it had neglected. For Virginia , her sister's endeavour was more direct but much less complex than her own. The quality that she most often attributes to painting (and, by extension, to Vanessa) is simplicity. It is likely that the position that literature is complex and painting simple could be easily disputed, particularly by a painter. Still, it remains that Virginia Woolf, like most artists and critics, was alive to the complexities of her own art and considered the other arts elementary in comparison. In her letters to painters and musicians, she professes to envy their directness; in her diaries, however, she can be quite dismissive: 'The devilish thing about writing is that it calls upon every nerve to hold itself taut. That is exactly what I cannot do – Now if it were painting or scribbling music or making patchwork quilts or mud pies, it wouldnt' matter' (*D2*, p. 129). Similarly, her belief that literature is the most self-conscious of the arts was, no doubt, influenced by the copious reading and writing which had refined her appreciation of literature '*as* literature' (*D2*, p. 120).

Like T. S. Eliot, Virginia Woolf recognised that individual talent must be measured against the complex background of the English literary tradition. She departed from Eliot, however, in her belief that the novel was the form most sensitive to historical events and most fitted to effect a rebellion. Although it could be argued that she held this opinion because the novel was the means of her own rebellion, literary theorists are often drawn to the same conclusion. Walter Reed argues that the novel, by its very name, encourages the critic to view it as 'inherently anti-traditional'.[6] For Virginia Woolf, the novel was the genre of the present moment. This should not be confused with the agelessness she attributes to poetry when she remarks that 'The poet is always our contemporary' (*E2*, p. 6). The novel represents a historical present, dependent on the past, anticipating the future.[7] It remains, therefore, in a constant state of flux. As the 'most pliable of all forms' (*RO*, p. 116), the novel is also the form most adapted to the combination and compromise that Virginia Woolf advocated in human relations.

LITERATURE AMONG THE ARTS

(i) The Attraction to Painting

In the defence of literature, Virginia Woolf seems to have been her own most rigorous opponent. Her advocacy is difficult to detect, as it is hidden beneath many professions of dissatisfaction and envy for artists in other media. Her particular awareness of the painter's opportunities is to expected, when one considers her milieu. It is evident not only in her essays on actual painters but also in her creation of fictional ones. In her letters and diaries, many metaphors are derived from painting: there are references to backgrounds, foreground, canvases, portraits, sketches and frames. Several descriptions are prefixed 'If I were to paint this.' Such evidence has prompted some critics to see her works as, if not literary equivalents to paintings, attempts to fulfil in her own medium the criteria developed by Clive Bell and Roger Fry for the visual arts. As a consequence, Virginia Woolf's writings have been interpreted in terms of their use of colour, space and significant form. Even more specifically, several critics have argued that Virginia Woolf was motivated by the desire to find a novelistic counterpart for Impressionism or Post-Impressionism, or both.[8]

Although Virginia Woolf's remarks often tempt the critic to consider her works in this light, such an approach can lead to various oversimplifications. In 'Pictures', she disparages those 'victims of the art of painting who paint apples, roses, china . . . as well as words can paint them, which is, of course, not very well' (*The Moment and Other Essays*, p. 140). Allen McLaurin, who has drawn some of the most suggestive and elaborate parallels between Fry's aesthetics and Virginia Woolf's novels, overemphasises the extent to which she tried to emulate the painter. In his discussion of 'those aspects of the novel [*The Waves*] which are more simply Impressionist',[9] McLaurin compares the novel's interludes to Monet's *Water Lilies*, since both register the quality of light from morning to sunset. Yet Virginia Woolf's reaction to Fry's description of Impressionism suggests that she found it elementary in comparison to writing: 'I've been given his book – a sumptuous book – in return for writing 200 addresses. I think it reads rudimentary compared with Coleridge. Fancy reforming poetry by discovering something scientific about the composition of light!' (*D2*, pp. 80–1). In his discussion of *Between the Acts* McLaurin proposes that 'holding up a broken mirror and other reflecting fragments is an attempt, perhaps, to capture the effect of Matisse's art as described by Fry'.[10] Admittedly, the similarity is striking. Fry wrote 'the world where a model sat on a carpet, in front of Matisse's easel, has been broken to pieces as though reflected in a broken mirror and then put together again into a more coherent unity'.[11] Yet in 1908, two years before she met Roger Fry, Virginia Woolf described the kind of unity she hoped to achieve in her writing in such a way as to anticipate the role of the shards of glass in *Between the Acts*: 'I attain a different kind of beauty, achieve a symmetry by means of infinite discords, showing all traces of the mind's passage through the world; achieve in the end, some kind of whole made of shivering fragments'.[12]

It also oversimplifies Virginia Woolf's aesthetic to identify it with Lily Briscoe's. Certainly many of Lily's dilemmas are analogous to those experienced by Virginia Woolf in writing. Still, it was noted that Virginia Woolf tended to underestimate the painter's task. Barbara Hardy's observation that 'James, like Lawrence, seems often to write about artists so that he may and yet need not be writing about novelists'[13] can be extended to Virginia Woolf and adapted to her critics: they may concentrate on analogies with paintings so that they may and yet need not address the difficulties presented by the literature itself.

Many of the qualities of Virginia Woolf's work which have been taken as evidence of her desire to imitate the painter could, more generally, be the product of her unusual susceptibility to visual appeals. In 'Walter Sickert: a Conversation' she observes that 'painting and writing have much to tell each other', and then continues, 'The novelist after all wants to make us see' (*E2*, p. 241). For Harvena Richter, Virginia Woolf's preoccupation with sight signifies the neglect and repression of her other senses:

> the few images of touch [in *The Waves*] are rendered visually . . .
> it could be said that Virginia Woolf . . . was anti-sensual,
> transforming sensory contact with the object into an intellectual-
> ized image or concept of it rendered in abstract or visual terms.[14]

Yet there is also evidence to suggest that seeing, for Virginia Woolf, was a tactile experience: 'what a little I can get down with my pen of what is so vivid to my eyes, & not only to my eyes: also to some nervous fibre or fan like membrane in my spine' (*D3*, p. 191). Richter argues that the intellectualisation of Virginia Woolf's other senses was due to her impulse to keep the world and its objects at bay so that they might serve as mirrors of the self. Her position appears to be supported by Virginia Woolf's observation that she seems to be 'hypnotised, as a child by a silver globe, by life' (*D3*,

p. 209). But Virginia Woolf immediately continues that she desires a closer relation, a more tactile understanding: 'I should like to take the globe in my hands & feel it quietly, round, smooth, heavy. & so hold it, day after day' (*D3*, p. 209).

Although the emphasis on sight in Virginia Woolf's works has, itself, been taken as further evidence of the extent to which she was influenced by painters, one could argue just as easily that it is the consequence of her philosophical reading. Richard Rorty describes the development of western philosophy as 'the story of the domination of the mind . . . by ocular metaphors'.[15] It was noted in Chapter 1 that Virginia Woolf's interest in creative perception was a result of her exposure to the work of G. E. Moore, whose association of perception with sight exemplifies Rorty's theory. Harvena Richter attributes Virginia Woolf's preoccupation with 'the angle of vision' to her reading of Moore.[16]

Another argument against viewing Virginia Woolf's writings as literary adaptations of paintings is that it was precisely the combination of the arts that appealed to her. Her desire was not to imitate the painter but to share his advantages while preserving her own. This eclecticism is in keeping with her vision of unity as assimilative rather than exclusive. She was attracted by the idea of a 'hybrid' artist [a term which she applied to Walter Sickert, who prided himself on being 'a literary painter' (*E2*, p. 243)]. In her critical essays, she suggests that certain writers were challenged by a divided allegiance – De Quincy, who tried to write poetry in prose, for example, or Hazlitt, who alternated between literature and painting.

The balance of different elements in a hybrid work of art is achieved by staying fairly close to the surface, by refusing to explore the depths of any one facet. Virginia Woolf remarked that *The Years*, her most heterogeneous novel, demanded a different kind of effort than *The Waves* 'because so many more faculties had to keep going at once, though none so pressed upon' (*D4*, p. 245). The diffusive, superficial quality of a hybrid work of art resembles that of the 'party consciousness' which clearly intrigued Virginia Woolf. Like Clarissa Dalloway, 'the perfect hostess', the hybrid artist sacrifices intensity in order 'to combine' (*MD*, p. 184). In her essay on Sickert, Virginia Woolf notes that the diverse nature of his art is reflected in his audience: 'he draws so many different people to look at his pictures' (*E2*, p. 243). This effect would be particularly valued by an artist who believed that the closest approximation to immortality was to be 'seen by many eyes' (*W*, p. 137).

In practice as well as in theory, then, Virginia Woolf insisted upon combination, which respects the thing in itself, rather than substitution, which dismisses it. Moreover, as the example of Walter Sickert reveals, the transference between literature and painting was not entirely one-way. Roger Fry also tried to turn aspects of literature to the painter's advantage. Much of the terminology in his essays on painting is derived from literary criticism: for example, he classified the visual arts under the headings 'Epic, Dramatic, Lyric, and Comedic' (*Vision and Design*, p. 230).

Although Virginia Woolf's desire to emulate the painter was qualified, the fact remains that she did try to appropriate some of his advantages. The 'divine gift of silence' (*E2*, p. 236) was probably the quality she most envied. Literature is composed of words (and, as it will be seen, Virginia Woolf's defence of literature is a defence of words). In her review of *Aspects of the Novel*, Virginia Woolf suggests that Forster's neglect of this fact is further evidence that the novel is not regarded as a work of art:

> though it is impossible to imagine a book on painting in which not a word should be said about the medium in which a painter works, a wise and brilliant book, like Mr Forster's, can be written about fiction without saying more than a sentence or two about the medium in which a novelist works. Almost nothing is said about words.   (*E2*, p. 54)

Often Virginia Woolf decried the awkwardness, the hypocrisy and the distortion of words. 'O Lord, protect and preserve us from words the defilers, from words the impure' (*BA*, pp. 221–2), the unanimous voice of the audience exclaims when Reverend Streatfield attempts a summing up in *Between the Acts*. Words are the vehicles of separation; they persist in making distinctions when, as Mrs Ramsay reflects, 'The real differences . . . are enough, quite enough' (*TL*, p. 19). As Reverend Streatfield prepares to speak, the audience realises the fragility of its connection: 'What need have we of words to remind us? Must I be Thomas, you Jane?' (*BA*, p. 222).[17]

The barrier erected by words can provide a refuge, yet this kind of screen making is culpable. As a child, Bernard relies on phrases to 'interpose something hard between myself and the stare of housemaids, the stare of clocks, staring faces, indifferent faces, or I shall cry' (*W*, p. 31). His strategy ensures that he need not uncover the source of his own emotions or those of others. 'We are all phrases in Bernard's story', Neville complains, 'He tells our story with extraordinary understanding, except of what we most feel' (*W*, p. 75). Painters are more direct, even when they turn to writing. Complimenting Dorothy Brett on her novel, Virginia Woolf wrote 'I think you get through, as painters do so often, the hide of words with your sincerity. Thats why I open and shut [your book] and see bright visions' (*L5*, p. 202).

Words may be obstructive and divisive but their principal fault is much humbler – they are inadequate; words fail. Lily Briscoe reflects upon their ineffectuality: 'Little words that broke up the thought and dismembered it said nothing. . . . Words fluttered sideways and struck the object inches too low' (*TL*, p. 274). The failure of words is felt most acutely when they are applied to painting. Virginia Woolf was aware of a disparity when she tried to describe her response to a painting by Sickert: 'the description is so formal, so superficial, that we can hardly force our lips to frame it; while the emotion is distinct, powerful, and satisfactory' (*E2*, p. 243). Mrs Swithin, challenged to discuss painting in *Between the Acts*, protests 'We haven't the words – we haven't the words. . . . Behind the eyes; not on the lips; that's all' (*BA*, p. 68). And although Bartholomew, the rationalist, then wonders, 'Thoughts without words. . . . Can that be?' (*BA*, p. 68), Virginia Woolf's writings often suggest that the best response is an inarticulate one (as if depth of feeling were inversely related to the ease of its expression). The comparative silence and social awkwardness of Terence and Rachel in *The Voyage Out* or Katharine and Ralph in *Night and Day* incline the reader to suspect the verbal facility of other characters.

A writer cannot avoid using words, but Virginia Woolf occasionally implies that he can achieve at least a relative silence by restraint. She intimates that just as those who respect the unknown are rewarded by those mysterious forces themselves, so the writer who refuses to pry and does not presume to explain the complexities of experience seems to be granted an extraordinary power of suggestion. Virginia Woolf considered Lytton Strachey's 'hint at force; at reserve; at the strength to leave things unsaid' (*D4*, p. 26) far superior to D. H. Lawrence's explicitness. Reading Jane Austen, she admired 'how definitely, by not saying something, she says it' (*E2*, p. 138). Similarly, in an essay on her father, she remembers Leslie Stephen's 'curious power to impress the scene' in such a way that the 'things that he did not say were always there in the background' (*E4*, p. 77).

The painter's ability to dispense with words is, however, only a negative advantage. Still, silence contributes to another aspect of painting that Virginia Woolf admired – its economy. 'I should only need a brush dipped in dun colour to give the tone of those eleven days. I should draw it evenly across the entire canvas', she wrote in her diary (*D1*, p. 239). In comparison with the directness of brush strokes, 'the process of language is slow & deluding. One must stop to find a word; then, there is the form of the sentence, soliciting one to fill it' (*D3*, p. 102). Virginia Woolf tried to approximate the painter's economy in her writing by suggesting that characters are best described by certain shapes and colours intuited by a perceptive observer. Ralph Denham's description of Katharine as a 'shape of light' (*ND*, p. 419), however vague, far surpasses the elaborate literary analogies of William Rodney. Lily Briscoe, who despairs of seeing Mrs Ramsay with fifty sets of eyes, nevertheless perceives the 'wedge-shaped core of darkness' which emerges only in solitude, when 'All the being and the doing, expansive, glittering, vocal, evaporated' (*TL*, p. 99).

The economy and immediacy of the painter's brush strokes have the additional advantage of making the unity of a work of art directly apprehensible. Touring Italy, Virginia Woolf was impressed by a fresco by Perugino: 'Each part has a dependence on the others; they compose one idea in his mind. That idea has nothing to do with anything that can be put into words.'[18] The sequential nature of literature prevented Virginia Woolf from achieving unity in the same manner. In this respect, however, it is doubtful whether she would have followed Perugino's example even if it had been possible to do so. It was after praising Perugino that she described her own method of creating 'symmetry by means of infinite discords . . . some whole made of shivering fragments'.[19] This kind of tenuous symmetry is in keeping with Virginia Woolf's inclusive vision. The reader may sense an undercurrent of distrust in her description of the unity Walter Sickert achieves in his paintings: 'whatever Sickert paints has to submit; it has to lose its separateness; it has to compose part of his scene' (*E2*, p. 239). Before considering the basis of her distrust, one should examine her response to music. For Virginia Woolf, music possessed the same advantages as painting but in a more extreme form. Correspondingly, her reservations about music were more acute.

(ii)   The Attraction to Music

In an attempt to prove that *The Years* is 'Virginia Woolf's *Twilight of the Gods*',[20] Jane Marcus observes

> The critics' failure to 'hear' Woolf's novels, although they 'see' them so well that they have concentrated on her ability to render words as painting, comes in part from ignoring the fact that her college was Covent Garden Opera House. Her Bayreuth essay expresses a longing to imitate music with words.[21]

As was noted earlier, it oversimplifies Virginia Woolf's work to see it as an imitation of another form of art, be it music or painting. Also, to maintain that her college was Covent Garden Opera House is to overlook a much more crucial educational resource – Leslie Stephen's library. Still, Marcus's attempt to redress the general neglect of the role of music in Virginia Woolf's writings is justified.[22] Virginia Woolf's friendship with Ethel Smyth heightened her awareness of music's potential, as did Leonard's purchase of a gramophone in the late 1920s: 'It occurred to me last night while listening to a Beethoven quartet that I would merge all the interjected passages into Bernard's final speech' (*D3*, p. 339). Yet, as Marcus suggests, Virginia Woolf's appreciation of music was not confined to her later years. Her first novel is ample evidence: Rachel Vinrace's musical talent is not an incidental feature of her character but its essence. From early in her career, as well, Virginia Woolf was intrigued by the listener's response to music: in *Jacob's Room* and elsewhere, she describes the variety of aesthetic attitudes represented by the audience of a musical performance.

In Virginia Woolf's discussion of the arts, painting usually provided the standard of comparison. Nevertheless, music can generally be depended upon to enter the conversation at some point. Certainly its terminology was pervasive. 'Rhythm' was such an integral term in Roger Fry's aesthetics (as in Forster's) that Clive Bell departs from his argument in *Art* to acknowledge it: 'I will never quarrel with that blessed word "rhythm".'[23] In her diary,

Virginia Woolf noted that she was 'writing The Waves to a rhythm not to a plot' (*D3*, p. 316). Often music is not invoked until the later stages of aesthetic discourse: for example, it appears only in the final pages of 'Walter Sickert: A Conversation'. The reason for this may be that music, which is removed from life, provides a vocabulary for comparisons among the arts, while ordinary language has no vocabulary to describe something so remote from its usual sphere.

In 'Impressions at Bayreuth', Virginia Woolf remarked 'how little words can do to render music' (*BP*, p. 21). Yet this does not deter a subjective response:

> The more beautiful a phrase of music is the richer its burden of suggestion, and if we understand the form but slightly, we are little restrained in our interpretations. We are led on to connect the beautiful sound with some experience of our own, or to make it symbolise some conception of a general nature. (*BP*, p. 21)

In the diary she kept in 1915, however, Virginia Woolf vowed to refrain from describing music since her efforts were too impressionistic: 'all descriptions of music are quite worthless, & rather unpleasant; they are apt to be hysterical, & to say things that people will be ashamed of having said afterwards' (*D1*, p. 33). This resolution would have been applauded by Clive Bell and Roger Fry, who believed that interpreting music or painting subjectively is the sign of an inadequate aesthete. In *The Years*, Kitty has an intense experience when *Siegfried* reawakens a passion she had repressed over many years. Even so, when the opera is over, she envies another member of the audience who had responded to the music alone:

> Kitty turned to the young man in her box. He was leaning over the ledge. He was still clapping. He was shouting 'Bravo! Bravo!' He had forgotten her. He had forgotten himself.
>
> 'Wasn't that marvellous?' he said at last, turning round.
>
> There was an odd look on his face as if he were in two worlds at once and had to drawn them together.
>
> 'Marvellous!' she agreed. She looked at him with a pang of envy. (*Y*, pp. 199–200)

Like painting, music not only dispenses with words but draws attention to their ineffectuality. Music is obviously not a silent art, but it relies on the possibility of silence. Silence is a necessary condition of painting, but in music it provides the significant contrast. In *Between the Acts*, Virginia Woolf tried to approximate music's more sophisticated use of silence. Her strategy is most explicit in the several references to 'making silence add its unmistakable contribution to talk' (*BA*, p. 50). A more subtle evocation of silence is created by the number of unheeded words and gestures. Twice Isa taps on the window to her children and twice 'it went unheeded' (p. 38). She, in turn, cannot hear the sounds that inhabit their innocent garden world: 'The drone of the trees was in their ears; the chirp of birds; other incidents of garden life, inaudible, invisible to her in the bedroom, absorbed them' (p. 20). And if silence can intervene between mother and child, it can easily thwart the communication between an artist and his audience. Throughout the pageant, the reader, with the audience, tries to make sense of songs and recitations when half the words are 'blown away' (p. 96). When 'even the great words became inaudible' (p. 165) and the audience is no longer able to comply with the illusion, Miss La Trobe's suffering is acute: '"This is death," she murmured, "death"' (p. 165). But just as a pause in music makes the listener sensitive to the softest note, the repeated failures to hear in *Between the Acts* intensify even the most trivial moments of communication: '"All that fuss about nothing!" a voice exlaimed. People laughed. The voice stopped. But the voice had seen; the voice had heard. For a moment Miss La Trobe behind her tree glowed with glory' (p. 163).

Music also shares the enviable economy of painting. In *The Voyage Out*, Rachel tells Terence 'You ought to write music. Music, you see . . . music goes straight for things. It says all there is to say at once. With writing it seems to me there's so much . . . scratching on the match-box' (*VO*, p. 251). If words are circuitous, it is at least partly because they are burdened with associations. In his efforts to make words accessible to Rachel, Terence suggests that she consider only the sound of a passage from Milton. But, for Rachel, the words are 'laden with meaning'. She 'could not keep her attention fixed upon them, but went off upon curious trains of thought suggested by words such as "curb" and "Locrine"' (*VO*, p. 399).

Perhaps words can approach the condition of music and painting when they restrict themselves to the most basic of human conditions, when they abandon all sophistications and refinements and are concerned only with unanalysable instincts. The old crone's 'ancient song' in *Mrs Dalloway*, which is almost impossible to decipher, 'of love – love which has lasted a million years' (*MD*, p. 123) may be such an approximation. But later, at Clarissa's party, Mrs Hilbery will maintain that 'songs without words' are 'always the best' (p. 288). In *Between the Acts*, Isa also attempts to reduce language to the primal story: 'love; and hate. . . . All else was verbiage, repetition' (*BA*, pp. 109–10).

Virginia Woolf was especially attracted by the simultaneity of music. She felt that if she found a way to transpose the resonance of a chord to literature, it might be possible to fulfil her object – to give the moment whole: 'I should like to write four lines at a time, describing the same feeling, as a musician does; because it always seems to me that things are going on at so many different levels simultaneously' (*L5*, p. 315). Perhaps Beethoven's quartets, which inspired the final section of *The Waves*, also prompted her to develop a theory of the four levels of existence while working on her next novel, *The Years*: 'I have now reached a further stage in my writers advance. I see that there are 4? dimensions; all to be produced; in human life; & that leads to a far richer grouping & proportion: I mean: I: & the not I: & the outer & the inner' (*D4*, p. 353). In *The the Lighthouse*, metaphors are drawn from harmony and counterpoint: the Ramsays' marriage is compared to 'two notes sounding together' (*TL*, p. 65), and the story of the fisherman and his wife complements the events in the Ramsay household 'like the bass gently accompanying a tune' (p. 91).

Although music is sequential, it conveys a greater sense of unity than most forms of literature because, conventionally, its movements are more clearly patterned and its resolutions, though delayed, are inevitable. For Rhoda in *The Waves*, music provides a reassuring sense of solidity:

> There is a square; there is an oblong. The players take the square and place it upon the oblong. They place it very accurately; they make a perfect dwelling-place. Very little is left outside. The structure is now visible; what is inchoate is here stated; we are not so various or so mean; we have made oblongs and stood them upon squares. This is our triumph; this is our consolation. (*W*, pp. 176–7)

This unity is quite unlike the kind envisaged by Virginia Woolf for her own art: in fact, she was pointed in her departure from the harmonious resolutions provided by music, describing her desired effect as a 'symmetry by means of infinite discords'.[24] Although critics often assume that Virginia Woolf shared Rhoda's sense of music's triumph and consolation, there is evidence that her attitude towards music was quite ambivalent.

(iii) Reservations

E. M. Forster is among the critics who suggest that Rhoda's response to the string quartet represents Virginia Woolf's own.[25] Yet the effect she describes is very different from Forster's own reaction to music. In *Aspects of the Novel*, he advises the novelist to follow music's liberating example:

> Expansion. That is the idea the novelist must cling to. Not completion. Not rounding off but opening out. When the symphony is over we feel that the notes and tunes composing it have been liberated, they have found in the rhythm of the whole their individual freedom. Cannot the novel be like that?[26]

In contrast, Rhoda's conception of music is clearly one of 'completion' and 'rounding off'. The music evokes geometrical shapes which in Virginia Woolf's writings generally suggest protective boundaries: it becomes a 'perfect dwelling-place'. As in 'The String Quartet', *The Voyage Out* and elsewhere, music is described in terms of architecture. The effect of both forms of art is, at once, ennobling and alienating. They inspire dedication to a vision of art and progress which is realised in so far as it neglects the individual. The disparity between our response to architecture and its obliviousness to human concerns is commented upon in *Jacob's Room*: the Parthenon 'exists quite independently of our admiration. Although the beauty is sufficiently humane to weaken us, to stir the deep deposit of mud – memories, abandonments, regrets, sentimental devotions – the Parthenon is separate from all that' (*JR*, p. 242). In many respects, the silent painting, the string quartet and the Parthenon, as portrayed by Virginia Woolf, are representatives of art divorced from life. They can be seen as the products of the rigorous application of the principles of framing.

Their unity depends upon exclusivity and the imposition of balanced proportions. A musician himself, Forster did not consider music to be so remote from life. He saw it as a way of overcoming boundaries and the artificiality of beginnings and endings. For Virginia Woolf, music had the opposite effect: the dwelling-place that the string quartet erects in *The Waves* is the Palace of Art.[27]

That Virginia Woolf saw the formal perfection and sense of completion that music achieves as the product of framing is reinforced by another aspect of Rhoda's image of the string quartet. The square is placed within the oblong; 'very little is left outside'. It has, in effect, created a frame. In *La Vérité en peinture*, Derrida maintains that Kant, in the effort to purify beauty, is left with only the frame – paradoxically, the essence of art:

> Take away from a painting all representation, signification, theme, text as intended meaning, take away also all the material . . . take away its background . . . and what is left? The frame, the framing, a play of forms and lines which are structurally homogeneous with the structure of the frame.[28]

It would seem that the tendency of the frame to disappear is complemented by its capacity to absorb. The same effect is created when the surroundings that had framed Mrs Ramsay are, after her death, revealed to be 'like curves and arabesques flourishing round a centre of complete emptiness' (*TL*, p. 275).

As early as 'Impressions at Bayreuth', there are indications that Virginia Woolf resented the aloofness of music: 'Ecclesiastical music is too rigidly serene and too final in its spirit to penetrate as the music of *Parsifal* penetrates' (*BP*, p. 19). Even in opera itself, where the remoteness of music is tempered by a story, Virginia Woolf observes, 'accustomed as one is to find the explanation of a drama in the love of man and woman, or in battle, one is bewildered by a music that continues with the utmost calm and intensity independently of them' (*BP*, p. 19). Paradoxically, the consolation that the music affords Rhoda in *The Waves* is a result of this obliviousness. In *Mrs Dalloway*, music is shown to have a calming effect when it is heard in the rooms of the suffering and the dying. But the comfort it offers is due to its indifference to human fate, to the fact that it remains unaffected by the insignificant claims of the individual:

had some woman breathed her last, and whoever was watching, opening the window of the room where she had just brought off that act of supreme dignity, looked down on Fleet Street, that uproar, that military music would have come triumphing up to him, consolatory, indifferent.

It was not conscious. There was no recognition in it of one's fortune, or fate, and for that very reason even to those dazed with watching for the last shivers of consciousness on the faces of the dying, consoling. (*MD*, pp. 208–9)

In response to the 'unmixed beauty' (*ND*, p. 441) of music, Virginia Woolf felt impelled to supply the shrill, discordant noise of life and the present moment. The formal perfection of music is akin to Mrs Ramsay's beauty – so remote as to alienate a more authentic response to the total human being: 'Beauty had this penalty – it came too readily, came too completely. It stilled life – froze it' (*TL*, p. 273). To pursue this beauty is, finally, an evasion, 'for beauty offers her lures, has her consolations' (p. 208) which deflect her admirers from the truth. They are the victims of 'the deceptiveness of beauty' in which 'all one's perceptions, half-way to truth, were tangled in a golden mesh' (p. 82). The supremacy of such deceptive beauty is threatened when Eleanor Pargiter hazards the judgment 'Beautiful?' in response to the garbled children's song in the final chapter of *The Years* (*Y*, p. 465). The classical music at the end of the pageant in *Between the Acts* must be united with the anonymous bray of the megaphone if it is to represent 'ourselves'.

For Clive Bell, music's lack of human reference was an unqualified advantage. Poetry, he maintained, could never attain 'that remote aesthetic beatitude in which, freed from humanity, we are upstayed by musical and pure visual form'.[29] To a lesser degree, Roger Fry also feared the contamination of human reference. Virginia Woolf remarked upon his desire for 'art to be art; literature to be literature; and life to be life' (*E4*, p. 90). Despite his interest in hybrids, Fry often seemed to protect the integrity of his own art, preferring a painterly work of literature to a literary painting. In a review of an exhibition by Survage, he observes, 'Survage is almost precisely the same thing in paint that Mrs Woolf is in prose'.[30] But having acknowledged his partiality to Virginia Woolf's prose, Fry admits 'a rather strong distate for Survage's visual statements'.[31] After Virginia Woolf published her article on Walter Sickert, Fry told her 'you wouldn't find any literature in my paintings' (*L5*, p. 256).

The extent to which Fry and Bell valued purity is evident from their desire to align art with mathematics. In 'Some Questions on Esthetics', Fry maintains that it is difficult to distinguish an aesthetic response 'from the responses made by us to certain abstract mental constructions such as those of pure mathematics. Here I conceive the emotional states due to the apprehension of relations may be extremely similar to those aroused by esthetic appreciation'.[32] Or in Bell's words, 'Art transports us from the world of man's activity to the world of aesthetic exaltation. . . . The pure mathematician rapt in his studies knows a state of mind which I take to be similar, if not identical'.[33] Virginia Woolf was not immune to the appeal of artistic purity, but she was conscious of the threat it posed to literature. In *Night and Day*, Katharine Hilbery is attracted by a primarily aesthetic image of mathematics which, like Rachel Vinrace's music, is set in opposition to the circumlocutions of literature:

> in her mind mathematics were directly opposed to literature. She would not have cared to confess how infinitely she preferred the exactitude, the star-like impersonality, of figures to the confusion, agitation, and vagueness of the finest prose. (*ND*, p. 40)[34]

Since Bell, Fry and Virginia Woolf often, if only temporarily, modified their opinions in deference to one another, it is sometimes difficult to isolate a clear point of contention among them. All three had, on occasion, condemned the impurity of words, yet each meant something different by the charge. In *Between the Acts*, 'words the impure' are so named because, in their inadequacy, they distort experience. Clive Bell, on the other hand, felt words were tainted by their association with humanity and, thus, could never be the medium of pure art: 'Literature is never pure art. Very little literature is a pure expression of emotion; none, I think, is an expression of pure inhuman emotion'.[35] Roger Fry's intermediary position is expressed in a letter he wrote to Virginia Woolf:

> you're the only one now Henry James is gone who uses language as a medium of art, who makes the very texture of the words have a meaning and quality really almost apart from what you are talking about. Nearly all the other good writers have

something of rhetoric however hidden beneath reserve and good taste.[36]

In a diary entry, Virginia Woolf seems to share Fry's opinion: 'Art is being rid of all preaching: things in themselves: the sentence in itself beautiful' (*D4*, p. 126). In both statements, however, two criteria for purity in language are conflated: the absence of 'rhetoric' or 'preaching' and the subordination of all other concerns to the beauty inherent in language itself, the 'texture' of words. Virginia Woolf's remark must be placed within its context – an attack on D. H. Lawrence – which would suggest that her complaint was primarily against 'preaching'. Fry, whose position was no doubt tempered by the fact that he was writing to Virginia Woolf, concentrates on the 'texture' of words which, he maintains, can be considered 'almost apart from what you are talking about'. In this respect, he approaches the position implicit in Clive Bell's *Art* that the aesthetic potential of language is inversely related to its representational function:

> I know how little the intellectual and factual content of great poetry has to do with its significance. The actual meaning of the words in Shakespeare's songs, the purest poetry in English, is generally trivial or trite. They are nursery-rhymes or drawing-room ditties.[37]

The nursery rhymes in *Between the Acts* might lead one to assume that Virginia Woolf hoped to achieve the purity admired by Bell. During the recitation of 'A Song of Sixpence', however, the human reference is merely transferred from the words to the voice:

And the voice that wept for human pain unending said:

> *The King is in his counting house,*
> *Counting out his money,*
> *The Queen is in her parlour*   (*BA*, p. 211)

The effect is quite the opposite of the one Bell intended. The triviality of the words is not due to their subordination to formal considerations. Instead, the implication of this passage is that words generally provide such inadequate expressions of our

thoughts and feelings that they might as well confine themselves
to nursery rhymes.

(iv)   The Defence of Words

Since it is the nature of its medium – words – which provides the
grounds for the case against literature, the defence of literature is,
necessarily, a defence of words. Virginia Woolf's frustration with
the inadequacy of words may be taken as evidence of her intuition-
ism or irrationalism.[38] Yet it could be argued that, despite her
frequent complaints, she granted language almost mystical powers
of penetration. 'One always sees the soul through words', she
maintains in her diary (*D2*, p. 184). And, in 'Craftsmanship', she
observes that, although words are employed to do otherwise, they
continually betray the personality of their authors: 'Why words do
this, how they do it, how to prevent them from doing it nobody
knows. They do it without the writer's will; often against his will'
(*E2*, p. 248). The clichés in *Between the Acts* seem embarrassingly
inaccurate at first, but their meanings continue to expand until
finally they are shown to encompass a great deal of the truth. Mrs
Swithin's 'divided glance' (*BA*, p. 14) and her brother's exasperated
complaint that she had not 'fixed her gaze' (p. 32) create a more
suggestive dialectic than that between intuition and reason, or
inclusion and exclusion. Also, the silence that Virginia Woolf
wished to approximate need not be equated with wordlessness.
In 'Hours in a Library', she maintains that reading nourishes our
'silent life' (*E2*, p. 37). And Terence Hewet, in *The Voyage Out*,
defines silence as 'the things people don't say' (*VO*, p. 262).
    The impurity, the spontaneity, the awkwardness and the circum-
locution of words, while they may vex the writer, affirm a
connection with life. In 'Walter Sickert: A Conversation', it is
intimated that, although words are not as restrained a medium as
brush strokes, they have a living quality that paint and brush
strokes lack. Language lends itself to personification. Talk 'runs
hither and thither, seldom sticks to the point' (*E2*, p. 233). When
words simplify they also intensify: 'love; and hate. . . . All else
was verbiage, repetition' (*BA*, pp. 109–10). But the simplification
of painting involves a renunciation. While Virginia Woolf professed
to admire the painter's economy, she also noted that it is gained
at the expense of subtlety: 'painters lack sub[t]lety; there were

points of light, shades beneath the surface' (*D1*, p. 239). There is a suggestion in 'Walter Sickert: a Conversation' that painting is a powerful but essentially primitive medium. The observer must abandon his other senses and the associative processes of his mind in order to become 'all eye' (*E2*, p. 235). This requires an effort that is soon exhausted: 'the eye can hold no more; it shuts itself in sleep' (*E2*, p. 235). As Bernard says in the art gallery, 'I am yawning. I am glutted with sensations. I am exhausted with the strain' (*W*, pp. 170–1). This movement towards sleep intensifies the sense of death associated with the art gallery, where one steps outside 'the sequence of things' (*W*, p. 168). Fittingly, Bernard hastens there to observe his funeral service for Percival. Yet it is not long before he is eager to return to life and humanity: 'I want life round me, and books and little ornaments, and the usual sound of tradesmen calling on which to pillow my head after this exhaustion' (*W*, p. 171). Consequently, to Clive Bell's censure of the impurity of literature, Virginia Woolf counters 'Lord I'm glad I'm not a painter – their taste is so pure; theres no getting round them' (*L5*, p. 8).

Music's imperviousness to the living medium of words has sinister reverberations as well. Virginia Woolf's enthusiastic response to *Parsifal* in 'Impressions at Bayreuth' is partly due to her conviction that in Wagner's opera 'the words are continued by the music so that we hardly notice the transition' (*BP*, p. 19). In this early essay Virginia Woolf describes the satisfaction afforded by Wagner as 'that sense of answer which the finest art supplies to its own questions'. (*BP*, p. 19). These comments may be compared to a short story, 'The String Quartet', written after Virginia Woolf became aware of the inadequacy of her impressionistic response to music. For the most part, the story consists of the subjective impressions of the narrator during a string quartet. The self-conscious listener, however, realises she has indulged a weakness: 'That's the worst of music – these silly dreams. The second fiddle was late, you say' (*HH*, p. 30).[39] The satisfaction Virginia Woolf experienced at *Parsifal* when music seemed to answer its own questions is subverted in this story. The narrator enters the concert hall with a question hovering at the edge of articulation:

if it's all the facts . . . that come to the surface – what chance is there?

Of what? It becomes every minute more difficult to say why, in spite of everything, I sit here believing I can't now say what, or even remember the last time it happened. (*HH*, pp. 27–8)

But the music does not answer her question, it silences it: 'Ask what? Remain unsatisfied? I say all's been settled; yes; laid to rest under a coverlet of rose leaves, falling. Falling' (*HH*, p. 29). Like Bernard in the art gallery, the narrator is drawn to images of sleep and death. The purity of the string quartet is so complete and impersonal that afterwards the narrator finds herself craving human intercourse:

Bare are the pillars [erected by the music in her imagination]; auspicious to none; casting no shade; severe. Back then I fall, eager no more, desiring only to go, find the street, mark the buildings, greet the applewoman, say to the maid who opens the door: A starry night. (*HH*, pp. 31)[40]

The answer that is laid to rest by the string quartet is one of several buried words and hidden messages alluded to in Virginia Woolf's writings. During Bernard's visit to the art gallery, he too is conscious that 'Something lies deeply buried. For one moment I thought to grasp it' (*W*, p. 170). Although the narrator in *A Room of One's Own* refuses to supply her audience with 'a nugget of pure truth' (*RO*, p. 6), she does suggest that her lecture contains a message that she 'will not trouble you with . . . now, though if you look carefully you may find it for yourselves in the course of what I am going to say' (*RO*, p. 9). The hidden message cannot be delivered prematurely; its revelation requires patience, diligence and respect. Similarly, the buried word, given time, will germinate. Bernard realises that he cannot force his intimation: 'But bury it, bury it; let it breed, hidden in the depths of my mind some day to fructify' (*W*, p. 170). In a less direct, and obviously less doctrinal, manner than Eliot, Virginia Woolf also suggests that redemption lies in the resurrection of the word through love. The new language that Bernard craves in the final section of *The Waves* is 'a little language such as lovers use' (*W*, p. 323). When, in *Between the Acts*, William Dodge succeeds, after several abortive attempts, in saying 'I'm William' to Mrs Swithin, he means the words to convey the full extent of his gratitude and devotion. And, miraculously, they do:

'Mr . . .' she began.

'I'm William,' he interrupted.

At that she smiled a ravishing girl's smile, as if the wind had warmed the wintry blue in her eyes to amber. (*BA*, p. 89)

THE NOVEL AMONG THE GENRES

(i) The Generic Spectrum

The range of the varieties of literature, like that of the different forms of art, tempted Virginia Woolf with the possibilities of combination. And while aspects of other arts can be transposed to literature only metaphorically, one can mix genres quite literally, and Virginia Woolf did so in poetic novels, fantastic biographies and epistolary essays. She often used the term 'novel' as a catchall: in 'The Narrow Bridge of Art', she envisages the novel of the future: 'It will have something of the exaltation of poetry, but much of the ordinariness of prose. It will be dramatic, and yet not a play' (*E2*, p. 224). While the essayist predicted the emergence of such a hybrid, the diarist claimed it as her own: 'I think it must be something in this line. . . . Away from facts: free; yet concentrated; prose yet poetry; a novel & a play' (*D3*, p. 128).

Such an objective may not seem revolutionary today: the study of genre has demonstrated not merely the possibility but the inevitability of generic multiplicity. That this circumstance requires continued demonstration, however, is evidence of the persistence of generic purists. And while, in the twenties, many writers were experimenting with a variety of combinations, literary critics, having succeeded in shifting the focus of critical attention from the writer's life to his works, were trying to establish the contours of each genre. Although the reception of *The Craft of Fiction* (1921) was varied, Percy Lubbock's argument that the writer must remain within the confines of the appropriate form was influential. The disparity between the writer and the critic is illustrated by Virginia Woolf herself, who tried to put 'everything' into her novels, and yet in her critical essays frequently portrayed the writer as having to choose between mutually exclusive alternatives. The choice is not necessarily represented as one among different genres; more often, it involves consistency to a particular 'world', 'truth' or 'reality': 'One could number on one's fingers half a dozen novels which set out to be masterpieces and yet have failed because the belief flags; the realities are mixed' (*E2*, p. 59). As a writer, Virginia Woolf admired Harold Nicolson's attempt to mix 'the truth of real life' and 'the truth of fiction' in *Some People*, while, as a critic, she maintained that 'both truths . . . are antagonistic; let them meet and they destroy each other' (*E4*, pp. 233–4).

Clearly such hybrids require sensitivity. The combinations they effect must be aesthetically satisfying: mere multiplicity is not its own justification. Roger Fry admired *Carmen* because of the symmetry with which it combined the various arts: 'It exactly illustrates my theory of the mixture of the arts. For it's almost perfect – the music never so important that you want to think of it as music and yet always adequate to the situation' (quoted in *RF*, pp. 275–6). Virginia Woolf was particularly aware of the necessity of achieving balanced proportions while writing *The Pargiters* which was to combine 'facts' and 'the vision' and to include 'satire, comedy, poetry, narrative' (*D4*, pp. 151–2). Although *The Pargiters* could not withstand the strain, its failure suggested a new method of combination: Virginia Woolf maintained that its two descendants – *The Years* and *Three Guineas* – are, in fact, 'one book' (*D5*, p. 148). Similarly, while writing *Between the Acts*, she envisaged a book of criticism which, like the novel, would provide a summary of English literature.

In Virginia Woolf's critical writings, the attempt to establish generic distinctions usually collapses into a comparison between prose and poetry. The shift is made quite explicitly in 'Notes on an Elizabethan Play':

> We have been comparing the play with prose, and the play, after all, is poetry.
> The play is poetry, we say, and the novel prose. Let us attempt to obliterate detail, and place the two before us side by side, feeling, so far as we can, the angles and edges of each. (*E1*, p. 58)

In many respects, the relationship between prose and poetry resembles that between literature and the other arts. Just as some critics suggest that Virginia Woolf created literary equivalents of paintings, others maintain that her works are attempts to write poetry in prose.[41] The latter approach is encouraged by the fact that Virginia Woolf's defence of prose, like her defence of literature, is hidden beneath many professions of envy and frustration.

Virginia Woolf admired the poet, as she did the painter, because his medium allows him to express himself with such economy: 'the compressions and elisions of poetry . . . mock the prose writer and his slow accumulations of careful detail' (*E*1, p. 218). Yet poets, too, lack subtlety: 'Forced by the nature of her medium, she [Elizabeth Barrett Browning] ignores the slighter, the subtler, the more hidden shades of emotion by which a novelist builds up touch by touch a character in prose' (*E*1, p. 217). The poet's economy also resembles the painter's in so far as it depends upon exclusivity. Virginia Woolf, however, desired inclusiveness: 'The poets succeeding by simplifying', she wrote in her diary, 'practically everything is left out. I want to put practically everything in; yet to saturate' (*D*3, p. 210).

In 'The Art of Fiction', Virginia Woolf explicitly aligns the poet with the painter and musician in opposition to the novelist. As was noted in Chapter 1, she defended the claims of art with unusual vigour in this essay because she was reacting to what she considered the parasitic servitude to life advocated by Forster in *Aspects of the Novel*. The novelist's allegiance to life is unfavourably compared to that of the poet, painter and musician to art:

> a novel . . . has roused a thousand ordinary human feelings in its progress. To drag in art in such a connection seems priggish and cold-hearted. It may well compromise the critic as a man of feeling and domestic ties. And so while the painter, the musician, and the poet come in for their share of criticism, the novelist goes unscathed. His character will be discussed; his morality, it may be his genealogy, will be examined; but his writing will go scot-free. There is not a critic alive now who will say that a novel is a work of art and that as such he will judge it. (*E*2, pp. 54–5)

Prose is 'debased by a thousand common uses' (*E*1, p. 172), whereas poetry, though not as aloof as music or painting, is at least more remote from everyday life than prose. The relative purity of language can also be determined by referring to the proposition that objects of aesthetic appreciation must be considered as ends in themselves rather than means. The novel, as portrayed in 'The Art of Fiction', is merely a means of revealing the character of the author, while the poem is judged as an end in itself.[42] Frank Lentricchia notes that Sartre in his essay 'What Is Literature?' also used the distinction between ends and means to differentiate between poetry and prose:

> [Sartre] labored to keep distinct . . . a Kantian aesthetic tradition with its celebration of an enclosed 'intransitive' sort of discourse which in its self-sufficiency does not take an object; and the tradition of engagement with its celebration of a transitive discourse.[43]

Or, in Virginia Woolf's less complicated formulation: 'prose has neither the intensity nor the self-sufficiency of poetry . . . it must be connected on this side and on that' (*E1*, p. 168).

Yet, if one assumes that Virginia Woolf preferred intransitive discourse, it is difficult to account for her attraction to letters as a genre. As was previously suggested, she was drawn to the epistolary form because it united author and audience. Letters are the paradigm of transitive discourse.[44] Indeed, Virginia Woolf distrusted prose when it abandoned its communicative function to pursue beauty: 'After all, what is a lovely phrase?' she wrote to Vita Sackville-West, 'One that has mopped up as much Truth as it can hold' (*L3*, p. 237). In the same way that she was prompted to counteract music's sublimity with life's discord, she felt impelled to supply the 'rasp'[45] of direct communication when confronted with the self-sufficiency of fine prose.

If Virginia Woolf remained ambivalent regarding the relative merits of poetry and prose it is because she also celebrated their differences. 'No critic', she observes, 'ever gives full weight to the desire of the mind for change' (*D4*, p. 145). Throughout her diary, she alternately craves poetry, novels and biography; each satisfies a different mood. Consequently, a scale, with biography at one extreme, poetry at the other and the novel fluctuating within the range provided, reflects Virginia Woolf's attitude more accurately than any simple opposition.[46] On occasion, she suggests that the two poles could be described as craft and art, facts and beauty, or even surface and depth. This scale is the prototype for another Virginia Woolf envisages, in which novels are ranged from the most realistic to the most poetic: 'For instance Defoe at one end: E. Brontë at the other. Reality something they put at different distances' (*D3*, p. 50).[47]

Yet such scales pose a threat to Virginia Woolf's all-inclusive vision. She was, therefore, drawn to paradoxes which would bring together the opposite poles: Orlando's biographer maintains that 'the most ordinary conversation is often the most poetic' (*O*, p. 228); in 'Robinson Crusoe', Virginia Woolf demonstrated the consummate artistry of Defoe's realism. She also encouraged the artist to withdraw until he found a perspective which would encompass both realism and beauty: in 'Notes on an Elizabethan Play', she defines 'the great artist' as 'the man who knows where to place himself above the shifting scenery' (*E1*, p. 55). While writing *The Pargiters*, she remarked that 'there's a good deal of gold – more than I'd thought – in externality' (*D4*, p. 133). Again, the image suggests that the artist's perspective must be altered. Accustomed to pursuing that which lies beneath appearances, he neglects the valuable material that the surface affords.

The absence of references to drama in the preceding discussion is a consequence of the ambiguous position it holds in Virginia Woolf's writings; in 'Notes on an Elizabethan Play', she maintains that the 'play is poetry' (*E1*, p. 58) while, on other occasions, she remarks that the dramatist's allegiance is to the surface rather than to the depths associated with poetry: 'This particular relation with the surface is imposed on the dramatist of necessity' (*D4*, p. 207). Though drama may be seen as a way of combining the advantages of both extremes of the generic spectrum, Virginia Woolf's few forays into playwriting were parodic. She was, however, drawn to the metaphors provided by drama. Like letters, plays are a transitive genre, and Virginia Woolf was particularly intrigued by the effects of an audience. In a letter to George Rylands, she remarks that novelists, beginning with George Eliot, 'lost the sense of an audience' and, consequently, were deprived of 'an abandonment, richness, surprise, as well as a redundancy, tedious-ness and superficiality'. She concludes, 'Perhaps we must now put our toes to the ground again and get back to the spoken word, only from a different angle' (*L5*, pp. 334–5).

The letter to Rylands was written during the composition of *The Years* which, Virginia Woolf observed, 'tends more & more, I think – at any rate in E. [Elvira, an early name for Sara] M. [Maggie] scenes – to drama' (*D4*, p. 168). In a letter to her niece, Angelica Bell, she wrote that she intended to make the end of *The Years* into a 'play for you to act' and, in the same letter, maintained that one must 'make plays in which people are like ourselves only heightened' (*L5*, pp. 444–5). Her resolution was prompted by her dissatisfaction with the recent performance of T. S. Eliot's *Murder in the Cathedral*. Yet there is a suggestion that, although she considered the play a failure, she recognised the importance of the attempt. Often her own writings reflect an impulse similar to the one that prompted Eliot to use verse in *Murder in the Cathedral*. In 'Poetry and Drama', Eliot outlines his objective:

> What I should hope might be achieved by a generation of dramatists having the benefit of our experience, is that the audience should find, at the moment of awareness that it is hearing poetry, that it is saying to itself: '*I* could talk in poetry too!' Then we should not be transported into an artificial world; on the contrary, our own sordid, dreary, daily world would be suddenly illuminated and transfigured.[48]

Virginia Woolf shared Eliot's desire to illuminate the daily world rather than to construct an artificial one. Both believed that this transfiguration could be achieved by the redemption of the spoken word. But, while Eliot intended to accomplish this task by demonstrating how closely poetry can approximate prose, Virginia Woolf took the opposite route, revealing the poetry inherent in prose.

Although there is considerable dialogue in the final chapter of *The Years*, the desire Virginia Woolf expressed to George Rylands to 'get back to the spoken word' was not generally fulfilled by means of conversations among her characters. At the same time that dialogic experimentation was at its height in the novels of Ivy Compton-Burnett, Virginia Woolf's use of direct speech was very sparing. Her return to the spoken word was, for the most part, accomplished more obliquely by the colloquial tone and conversational rhythms of her narrative voice. The lyrical potential of this voice is never more apparent than in the scene that concludes Mrs Ramsay's dinner party:

> And all the lives we ever lived and all the lives to be
> Are full of trees and changing leaves.

She did not know what they meant, but, like music, the words seemed to be spoken by her own voice, outside her self, saying quite easily and naturally what had been in her mind the whole evening while she said different things. She knew, without looking round, that every one at the table was listening to the voice saying:

> I wonder if it seems to you
> Luriana, Lurilee

with the same sort of relief and pleasure that she had, as if this were, at last, the natural thing to say, this were their own voice speaking.   (*TL*, pp. 171–2)

Although this passage describes an instance of the illumination that T. S. Eliot sought to achieve in which poetry is recognised as being the most 'natural thing to say', it effects another, more challenging, transfiguration: the beauty of an unknown poem is suddenly brought into relief by the surrounding prose which enhances its rhythms and enriches its meaning. The lyrical effect of the combination of the poetry and the prose far exceeds that of the poem itself.

The rarity with which Virginia Woolf employed spoken words is an indication of her sense of their efficacy. She felt that Henry James limited his dialogue so that he could use it to achieve 'a very high light' (*L5*, p. 335). Mrs Ramsay speaks hardly at all in *To the Lighthouse*, but her words are used to frame 'The Window', with the result that these two comments on the weather, which would seem in ordinary circumstances entirely banal, are transformed into revelations.

(ii)   The Most Pliable of All Forms

At the same time that Virginia Woolf attempted to collapse or to enclose the generic spectrum, she also sought the most advantageous position within it. It is not surprising that, in describing Virginia Woolf's technique, David Daiches is drawn to the image of a precarious balancing act: 'Grounded in prose, the novelist must lean as far towards poetry as is consistent with his maintaining contact with the earth.'[49] Daiches proposes that Virginia Woolf was attracted to poetry because, by creating a sense of simultaneity not possible in prose, it contributes to a realistic presentation of life: 'poetry can . . . convey the organization of different and even conflicting aspects of a situation simultaneously'.[50] But it could be argued that the impetus behind Virginia Woolf's conception of the poetic novel was, primarily, the desire to create beauty in so far as it does not exclude humanity. She opposed what she called the 'false anti-literariness' of D. H. Lawrence (*D4*, p. 95). In 'The Man Who Loved His Kind', she derides the sanctimoniousness of Prickett Ellis, who interprets his inability to appreciate art as evidence of his love for his fellow man. Lily Briscoe is repelled by the same trait in Charles Tansley: 'He was preaching brotherly love. And all she felt was how could he love his kind who did not know one picture from another' (*TL*, p. 302). When, in 'Phases of Fiction', Virginia Woolf describes the delicate balance that a novelist should achieve, she does not neglect the importance of design and order:

> For the most characteristic qualities of the novel – that it registers the slow growth and development of feeling, that it follows many lives and traces their unions and fortunes over a long stretch of time – are the very qualities that are most incompatible with design and order. It is the gift of style, arrangement, construction, to put us at a distance from the special life and obliterate its features; while it is the gift of the novel to bring us into close touch with life. The two powers fight if they are brought into combination. The most complete novelist must be the novelist who can balance the two powers so that the one enhances the other. (*E2*, p. 101)

Poetry, Virginia Woolf suggests, is a means to achieve the necessary 'distance from the special life'. Its value does not lie in the increased exactitude it might bring to a depiction of life, as Daiches maintains, but in its ability to give 'the outline rather than the detail' (*E2*, pp. 224–5). If 'the outline' represents Virginia Woolf's version of significant form, it is more democratic than Bell's: it is not the product of selective vision but of a large perspective. 'To sit cheek by jowl with our fellows cramped up together is distasteful, indeed repulsive', she comments in 'Impassioned Prose', 'But draw a little apart, see people in groups, as outlines, and they become at once memorable and full of beauty' (*E1*, p. 172).

The novel occupies an intermediary position on the generic scale and, within the range available to the novelist, Virginia Woolf mediates between the extremes represented by Emily Brontë and Defoe. Like Mrs Ramsay, she effects a compromise that may seem a mockery to purists but, from another point of view, achieves a difficult synthesis. The novel is the only genre that remains sufficiently close to life while it pursues beauty to provide the artist with an ideal vantage point. In 'A Letter to a Young Poet', she observes that the poet is generally unable to 'include Mrs Gape' (*E2*, p. 187), while, in a letter to Lytton Strachey, she remarks that the biographer 'can't get that shifting and muddling which produces atmosphere', adding, 'I daresay I'm really putting in a claim for the novel form' (*L2*, p. 205). In comparison to poetry and biography, the boundaries of the novel seem indeterminate: 'novel' is often used in default of a more precise term. Yet the novel's willingness to risk its own integrity in the attempt to be all-inclusive is the very quality which makes it so appropriate to Virginia Woolf's vision.[51] In a letter of rare unreserve to Gerald Brenan, she wrote 'though I try sometimes to limit myself to the thing I do well, I am always drawn on and on, by human beings, I think, out of the little circle of safety, on and on, to the whirlpools; when I go under' (*L2*, p. 600).

Of course, there is the possibility of self-deception. If the novel is impure, its supporters will celebrate the hybrid. If the novel itself is a compromise, then it is suited to a vision of compromise. If it is a loose and jagged structure, lacking the design and order of poetry, painting and music, then the novelist will prefer the tenuous symmetry of the splintered, transitory and human. Virginia Woolf would respond that such speculations indicate a lack of faith, not only in the novel, but in life itself: in 'Phases of Fiction', she concludes

> This would seem to prove that the novel is by its nature doomed to compromise, wedded to mediocrity. . . . But any such verdict must be based upon the supposition that 'the novel' has a certain character which is now fixed and cannot be altered, that 'life' has a certain limit which can be defined. (*E2*, p. 101)

On other occasions, Virginia Woolf used a different argument to defend the novel against such allegations: she maintains that the failure of the novel is proof of its integrity. The reader is not deceived by the novel, which exposes its weaknesses, but by poetry and biography, which both foster an illusion of authority. In the same letter to Gerald Brenan, she argues that beauty, which you say I sometimes achieve, is only got by the failure to get it; by grinding all the flints together; by facing what must be humiliation – the things one can't do – To aim at beauty deliberately, without this apparently insensate struggle, would result, I think, in little daisies and forget-me-nots – simpering sweetnesses. . . . But I agree that one must (we, in our generation must) renounce finally the achievement of the greater beauty: the beauty which comes from completeness. (*L2*, p. 599)

In pursuing what is bound to fail and renouncing complete beauty, Virginia Woolf reflects current critical attitudes rather than those of her time. In *The Craft of Fiction*, Lubbock assumes that the novelist strives to create a flawless fictive world: 'in the fictitious picture of life the effect of validity is all in all. . . . When the point of view is definitely included in the book . . . then every side of the book is equally wrought and fashioned'.[52] Yet, as Erich Auerbach argues in *Mimesis*, Virginia Woolf's narrative voice refuses to accept the mantle of omniscience or even the degree of certainty necessary to enclose the novel's perspective.[53] The presence of frustrated artists within her novels reinforces the failure to create enclosures. Deconstruction provides the appropriate metaphor: Virginia Woolf may be said to show 'the crumbling abyssal, nontotalizable edges of the story's frame'.[54]

Such deliberate failures (as Virginia Woolf described *The Years*) are at least partially redeemed by the self-consciousness they represent. Joan Bennett's criticism that Virginia Woolf 'breaks the illusion'[55] in 'Time Passes' and the interludes in *The Waves* seems naïve, particularly in light of Virginia Woolf's pointed attempts to expose the fragility of art's illusions.[56] The 'chuff, chuff, chuff' of the gramophone persistently reminds the audience of the pageant in *Between the Acts* of the presence of a more prosaic level of reality. In *Vision and Design*, Roger Fry observes that 'the imaginative life' is characterised by the simultaneous participation in an illusion and consciousness of it: 'When we are really moved at the theatres we are always both on stage and in the auditorium.'[57] Although Virginia Woolf often expressed the desire to re-create the immediacy of experience, there are also indications that, in some ways, she preferred the distance that self-consciousness affords. Her eagerness to 'catch' thoughts 'before they became "works of art"' (*D3*, p. 102) was restrained by an aesthetic sensibility which found the 'likeness of the thought . . . more beautiful, more comprehensible, more available, than the thought itself' (*E2*, p. 271). The tendency she attributed to Fry, to receive 'the impulse to create from the work of art rather than from the thing itself' (*RF*, p. 284), is equally applicable to the novelist who once described her 'own particular search – not after morality, or beauty or reality – no; but after literature itself' (*D1*, p. 214).

The distance between words and their referents may be considered a fault, but it is one that ensures that literature is inescapably self-conscious. As David Lodge observes, a literary text, unlike *trompe-l'œil* painting or imitative music, cannot be confused with the reality to which it refers. Throughout *Between the Acts*, the inadequacy of given names and descriptions is stressed – the guidebook's account of Pointz Hall, for instance, or character summations which are limited to the most obvious roles: 'The father of my children' (*BA*, pp. 19, 60), 'the stockbroker' (p. 19), 'old Oliver's married sister; a widow' (p. 12). But, as Robert Kiely points out, despite the shortcomings of such labels, 'by their very inadequacy, they reveal dimensions of character or art that require contrasts in order to be seen'.[58] And, if literature does not share the immediacy of music or painting, it can, at least, refer to it. Virginia Woolf often describes other forms of art and the responses they elicit in order to convey various levels of experience: 'The question is can I get at quite different layers by bringing in music & painting together with certain groupings of human beings' (*D4*, p. 347).

Although all literature is self-conscious, Virginia Woolf felt that the qualities which emphasise disparity and defy enclosure are most characteristic of the novel. She wrote to Stephen Spender: 'I agree that poetry makes statements; and perhaps the most important; but aren't there some shades of being that it cant state? . . . I spent last week describing the state of reading poetry together, and I dont think you could say that in poetry' (*L5*, p. 315). It could be argued in support of her belief in the novel's unique potential for self-consciousness that the form arose from an attempt to provide a perspective outside of the story itself. Victor Shklovsky argued that the novel developed from two ways of writing a series of tales – 'linking' and 'framing'.[59] And, as David Lodge points out, 'It would seem to be a general rule that where one kind of aesthetic presentation is embedded in another, the "reality" of the embedded form is weaker than that of the framing form.'[60] Virginia Woolf further recognised that frames beget frames: every framing form is, in its turn, an embedded form. As Jonathan Culler observes, 'any attempt to codify context can always be grafted onto the context it sought to describe, yielding a new context which escapes the previous formulation'.[61] In *Between the Acts*, Virginia Woolf blurs the boundaries between embedded and framing forms until the reader wonders whether it is fruitful to distinguish between them at all. To show that the most complex interpretation is, in fact, as limited as the simplest story, an author may place the key to the necessary perspective in an obvious detail of the narrative, hidden by its conspicuousness, like the frames within Virginia Woolf's novels.

3

Frames

The number of references to rooms and windows in Virginia Woolf's writings has prompted several critics to comment on their role as symbols of consciousness and perception.[1] Yet rooms and windows, together with mirrors and thresholds, also serve other purposes; notably, they draw attention to the artifice of the works in which they appear. A precedent for this strategy was set in the visual arts: the practice of portraying a door or a window within a painting is well established.[2] It is a self-conscious device, since the doors and windows can be seen as framing the scene they enclose just as they are framed by the borders of the painting. The conspicuous boundaries of the inside frames suggest that the outside frames are similarly restricted.[3] Virginia Woolf's desire to expose such limitations may be related to her sense of herself as an outsider. In her diary, she maintains that it is her 'outsider's vision' which enables her to see things 'composed & in perspective' (*D2*, p. 55). An outsider's alienation is counterbalanced by his increased self-awareness; he can see the frame as well as the scene it encloses. The frames in Virginia Woolf's writings encourage the reader to become an outsider as well.

While the continuities between inner and outer frames are suggestive, the differences between them are equally so. The way in which doors and windows accidentally frame their random contents emphasises the deliberate exclusivity of the frame of a painting. Virginia Woolf was particularly attracted to rooms, windows, thresholds and mirrors because they retain the advantages of the frame of a painting without its limitations. They create boundaries, but theirs are the boundaries of life rather than art. They are capable of conferring order and creating significant relationships, but they are not able to impose their own designs. Life is neither restricted nor distorted, but is free to come and go, within the boundaries they provide.[4]

The effect that Virginia Woolf hoped to achieve with the frames provided by life is illustrated by a scene in the final section of *The Years*. The debris of the nightlong party is juxtaposed with the

Pargiters, who compose a work of art against the frame provided by the window:

> There were the smeared plates, and the empty wine glasses; the petals and the bread crumbs. In the mixture of lights they looked prosaic but unreal; cadaverous but brilliant. And there against the window, gathered in a group, were the old brothers and sisters.
>
> 'Look, Maggie,' she whispered, turning to her sister, 'Look!' She pointed at the Pargiters, standing in the window.
>
> The group in the window, the men in their black-and-white evening dress, the women in their crimsons, golds and silvers, wore a statuesque air for a moment, as if they were carved in stone. Their dresses fell in stiff sculptured folds. Then they moved.   (*Y*, pp. 466–7)

This scene may be compared to an episode in *The Ambassadors* in which Henry James creates the effect of framing the random elements of life more directly, simply by commenting upon Strether's sense of being enclosed within a picture during his excursion to the French countryside. Every detail of Strether's situation is aesthetically satisfying. The afternoon passes without his having 'once overstepped the oblong gilt frame. The frame had drawn itself out for him, as much as you please'.[5] The picture is completed by his vision of a couple boating: 'It was suddenly as if these figures, or something like them, had been wanted in the picture, had been wanted more or less all day.'[6] Yet, as Barbara Hardy has observed,

> The figures are 'as if' wanted in the picture but they come to break down the picture's static composition, do not stay, like figures cut through by the frame, on the edge of the impressionist landscape. They continue to move, to come nearer and loom larger, they cease to be compositionally appropriate to the picture and become people.[7]

The 'oblong gilt frame' represents Strether's perception of life as art. It is broken, however, at the moment of his realisation that the couple in the boat are Chad and Madame de Vionnet. The deflation that Strether experiences as art is displaced by life coincides with his recognition that Chad and Madame de Vionnet's relationship is not, as he had convinced himself, merely the product of a Parisian education in culture and manners, but also an affair prolonged by the efforts of an older woman. The descent from the realm of art to the sordid arena of life affects Strether 'like some unprovoked harsh note'.[8] In *The Years*, on the other hand, Sara makes no attempt to view the party as if it were an aesthetic object. Instead, amid the debris, she glimpses the impressive outline of the group against the window. By making this revelation dependent upon the random background of the window frame, Virginia Woolf suggests that life need not submit to an ordering apparatus exclusive to art if it is to be aesthetically satisfying. In *The Ambassadors*, it seems that life must either conform to art or destroy it, whereas in *The Years*, life maintains its integrity even when it is perceived as art; it is enhanced, not replaced.

The references to rooms, windows, thresholds and mirrors in Virginia Woolf's writings serve to emphasise the interpenetration of life and art, and to reveal the artifice and the limitations of the process of ordering and selection necessary to art. Considered separately, however, these frames provided by life fulfill more specific objectives. For Virginia Woolf, each one had an independent range of associations. One can only appreciate the complexity of their roles by examining them individually.

ROOMS

As the titles *Jacob's Room* and *A Room of One's Own* indicate, Virginia Woolf encouraged the reader to reflect upon the role of rooms in her work. A closer examination of rooms is also prompted by her lengthy descriptions of empty rooms which are quite pointedly not settings for other centres of interest. Robert Kiely has noted that 'The repeated use of such descriptions – static, framed, complete in themselves, observed only by the narrator and reader – invites a different kind of attention.'[9] The explanation generally provided for Virginia Woolf's preoccupation with rooms is that they serve as metaphors for the mind. Yet, as S. P. Rosenbaum observes, 'Jacob's rooms are . . . where epistemology and poetics come together'; he cites Virginia Woolf's comment when she envisaged the form of the novel, 'Let us suppose that the Room will hold it together.'[10]

In comparison with windows, thresholds and mirrors, a room may seem to be an odd sort of frame. Nevertheless, it was not only in *Jacob's Room* that Virginia Woolf depended on a room (or, less frequently, a house) to hold her vision together. At the end of *The Years*, she wanted the reader to 'feel a wall made out of all the influences; & this should in the last chapter close round them' (*D4*, p. 347). She describes her method in *The Waves* as 'picking out things in the room & being reminded by them of other things' (*D3*, p. 259). In the introduction to the Modern Library edition of *Mrs Dalloway*, she remarks that their predecessors had 'built' the novel 'on the wrong plan' and, as a consequence, her idea was forced 'to secrete a house for itself' (*MD*, pp. vii–viii). Reciprocally, Virginia Woolf portrays the perceiver of a work of art taking shelter in the enclosure it creates. Outsiders, like Rhoda and Louis in *The Waves*, view art as a means of penetrating the inside: for Rhoda, the string quartet becomes 'a dwelling place' (*W*, p. 176).

In Virginia Woolf's novels, the room often represents a refuge; the outdoors is generally portrayed as dark and watery – characteristics that, to her, suggested psychological as well as physical chaos. References to the 'dark places of psychology' (*E2*, p. 108) and the 'deep waters' (*D3*, p. 112) of depression recur in her writing. The room establishes the boundaries which hold these uncontrollable forces at bay. When the candles are lit in the Ramsays' dining room, the party is encouraged to see itself within a secure fortress surrounded by perilous, watery darkness:

> here, inside the room, seemed to be order and dry land; there, outside, a reflection in which things wavered and vanished, waterily . . . and they were all conscious of making a party together in a hollow, on an island; had their common cause against that fluidity out there. (*TL*, pp. 151–2)

The room is one of many forms of the enclosure. In its most primitive state, as the 'bright red cave', the enclosure suggests the collective efforts of mankind in a hostile environment. Perhaps because of its communal lifestyle, Vanessa Bell's household at Charleston had, for Virginia Woolf, a 'red cave effect – red cave in the profound winter hollow' (*D4*, p. 3). In *Jacob's Room*, the narrator observes that letters, the symbols of man's attempt to create an enduring fabric from the ephemera of daily life, 'are written when the dark presses round a bright red cave' (*JR*, p. 151). More imposing structures represent more elaborate human achievements. In *The Waves*, Hampton Court provides Rhoda with a reassuring sense of the order imposed by art. The British Museum Reading Room is often portrayed in Virginia Woolf's work as a monument to the mind, its dome encircling the reader 'as if one were a thought in the huge bald forehead' (*RO*, p. 40). It is only half-mockingly that the narrator asks, in *A Room of One's Own*, 'If truth is not to be found on the shelves of the British Museum, where . . . is truth?' (*RO*, p. 39). In her diary, Virginia Woolf recognised the importance of the British Museum as a focus of associations: 'I shall spend my day at the British Museum. (This is one of those visual images, without meaning when written down, that conveys a whole state of mind to me)' (*D3*, p. 321). For E. M. Forster, she was, in this respect, a representative of the humanistic naïvety of a generation unable to foresee the effects of war: 'She belonged to an age . . . for whom the dome of the British Museum Reading Room was almost eternal.'[11] Yet Forster underestimated Virginia Woolf's awareness of the consequence of war. In 'Time Passes', although the references to war are muted, the nihilism it fostered is represented, appropriately enough, by the image of a degenerating house. The destruction of an enclosure reveals the fragility of human constructs and the transitoriness of human achievements. The image recurs in 'A Sketch of the Past', when Virginia Woolf describes her reaction to the deaths of her mother and her half-sister, Stella: 'But at fifteen to have that protection removed, to be tumbled out of the family shelter, to see cracks and gashes in that fabric, to be cut by them, to see beyond them – was that good?' (*MB*, p. 118).

Virginia Woolf often heightened the contrast between the enclosure and the outside world by setting a brightly lit room against a night sky. Light is essential to the sense of security within the enclosure. It is only when the candles are lit at Mrs Ramsay's dinner party that the characters feel that together they have reached a safe harbour. When the lamps are extinguished in 'Time Passes', the house is prey to 'the flood, the profusion of darkness' (*TL*, p. 196). The brightly lit enclosure is a twofold image of security since the enclosure is a symbol of man's solidarity, and the light represents the rationality which enables him to triumph over confusion.[12] The Platonic metaphor of the 'light' of knowledge, reason or consciousness, as it is variously expressed, is particularly suited to a writer who identified perception with sight. And, since perception is viewed as a creative act in Virginia Woolf's writing, light is often portrayed as an originator rather than merely an illuminator. Ralph Freedman has observed that in *The Waves* 'The rising sun differentiates and ultimately creates the forms it illuminates. . . . The idea of creation through growing light . . . is translated in the main sections of the novel into an idea of creation by apprehension.'[13]

Since Virginia Woolf considered it necessary to recognise the limits of our knowledge and to respect the unknown, she was attracted to images of intermittent light – street lamps or the beams of a searchlight or lighthouse. The revelations that these lights afford punctuate dark tracts of ignorance and oblivion. In 'The Searchlight', Mrs Ivimey excuses the many unanswered questions that are raised by her reminiscences with the observation that 'The light . . . only falls here and there' (*HH*, p. 120). When Jacob Flanders catches sight of Florinda with another man, 'The light from the arc lamp drenched him from head to toe' (*JR*, p. 152). Yet the narrator's interest in a couple Jacob passes on the street is thwarted because 'The street lamps do not carry far enough to tell us' (p. 131).

For the most part, Virginia Woolf did not differentiate between types of light. There are occasions, however, when she distinguishes between the light nature provides outside the enclosure and the controlled light within. The sun's light is associated with the remorseless exposure of truth, while candles and lamps foster illusions and circumscribe our world. In her discussion of *Mrs Dalloway*, Marilyn Samuels remarks 'In the daylight one sees what is really there, not what one assumes to be there.'[14] Pausing by an open window, Clarissa Dalloway is unmasked by 'the stare of this matter-of-fact June morning' and feels herself 'suddenly shrivelled, aged, breastless' (*MD*, pp. 47–8). The concentrated light within the enclosure creates perimeters in which man appears to dominate his surroundings, but the diffusive outdoor light diminishes his sphere. After a woman's suffrage rally, Virginia Woolf observed in her diary 'It was a very fine afternoon & through a glass door one could see the day light – a difficult light for speakers to speak down. So prosaic, reasonable, & unconcentrated' (*D1*, p. 125).

The light of day may be unflattering but, as Katharine Hilbery discovers in *Night and Day*, the 'light of illusion' within the enclosure is oppressive as well:

> The dream nature of our life had never been more apparent to her, never had life been more certainly an affair of four walls, whose objects existed only within the range of lights and fires, beyond which lay nothing, or nothing more than darkness. She seemed physically to have stepped beyond the region where the light of illusion still makes it desirable to possess, to love, to struggle. . . . She wished inconsistently enough that she could find herself driving rapidly through the street.   (*ND*, p. 373)

While Katharine's sense of life's triviality should not be accepted without qualification, her impulse to escape the drawing-room is sound. This is not merely because its lights and fires, like those in Plato's cave, foster an atmosphere of illusion; the enclosure itself reduces life to 'an affair of four walls'. There are few simple oppositions in Virginia Woolf's work. The enclosure is a fortress which protects us from the confusion of the outdoors, but it is also a prison constructed of conventions and illusions.[15] In 'The Moment: Summer's Night', the narrator, exhilarated by the windy night, returns to the predictable order of her home: 'we . . . enter the door, and the square draws its lines round us, and here is a chair, a table, glasses, knives, and thus we are boxed and housed, and will soon require a draught of soda-water and to find something to read in bed' (*E2*, p. 297). Inside, we become the elements of our own designs; 'boxed and housed', we are compelled to follow predictable patterns.

Although it may be threatening, the dark and watery world outside the enclosure is aligned with truth and reality. Even the 'deep waters' of depression have 'an edge . . . which I feel of great importance. . . . One goes down into the well & nothing protects one from the assault of truth' (*D3*, p. 112). Water is also connected with the creative process: in writing *The Waves*, Virginia Woolf felt she had netted her vision of the 'fin in the waste of waters' (*D4*, p. 10). Like the shocks described in 'A Sketch of the Past', after the initial sense of annihilation and despair, such visions provide the impetus for art.

Illuminated by the light of reason, protected and confined by its walls, the room is obviously a fit metaphor for the individual mind. Virginia Woolf found a correspondence between minds and rooms particularly suggestive: 'I like going from one lighted room to another, such is my brain to me; lighted rooms' (*D2*, p. 310). In her fiction as well, the connection is often explicit. Orlando's biographer, in pursuit of her subject, ascends 'the spiral stairway into his brain – which was a roomy one' (*O*, p. 17).

Virginia Woolf usually developed the metaphor: as the title *A Room of One's Own* suggests, she emphasised the autonomy represented by a room. Towards the end of the lecture she is quite direct: 'a lock on the door means the power to think for oneself' (*RO*, p. 160). A closed door may, however, represent a culpable exclusivity. Virginia Woolf criticised Coventry Patmore because he 'was content to state his principle and shut the door' (*BP*, p. 38). Yet if the room encourages independence, it also strengthens an awareness of the otherness of other people. Virginia Woolf considered it necessary to respect this difference and to share Clarissa Dalloway's sense of 'the miracle' and 'the mystery' inherent in the fact that 'here was one room; there another' (*MD*, pp. 192–3). It is this attitude which accounts for Eleanor Pargiter's otherwise curious satisfaction at the sight of an unfamiliar couple entering a house and shutting the door behind them: '"There," Eleanor murmured, as he opened the door and they stood for a moment on the threshold. "There!" she repeated, as the door shut with a little thud behind them' (*Y*, p. 469). [One of Virginia Woolf's early titles for *The Years* was *Other People's Houses* (*D4*, p. 6n).]

At times, however, the room of one's mind may seem to be as oppressive a place of confinement as the drawing-room in *Night and Day*. In her diary, Virginia Woolf complains of 'fidgets' because 'I know this room too well – this view too well – I am getting it all out of focus, because I cant walk through it' (*D2*, p. 134). Outside the pressure of identity is not so burdensome. Yet, as Virginia Woolf illustrates in 'Street Haunting', the exhilaration that accompanies an escape into the anonymity of the street eventually palls, and we find ourselves welcoming 'the old possessions, the old prejudices' (*E4*, p. 166). Maria DiBattista has observed that in *Mrs Dalloway* Virginia Woolf contrasted the dispersal of the self represented by the streets with the 'ritual isolation' of Clarissa's attic room.[16] The drawing-room, DiBattista continues, 'mediates between the public streets and the private rooms'.[17] It is doubtful, however, that Virginia Woolf considered the drawing-room the image of a successful reconciliation. In her writings, the drawing-room is generally associated with purely conventional behaviour which, if it mediates between public and private lives, does so at a very superficial level. Indeed, Virginia Woolf's tendency to associate certain places with distinct modes of existence may have its roots in her childhood, when the schism between her private and her social life had a physical analogue in the separation of the study and the drawing-room at 22 Hyde Park Gate: 'The division in our life was curious. Downstairs there was pure convention: upstairs pure intellect. But there was no connection between them' (*MB*, p. 135).

In 'Life and the Novelist', Virginia Woolf maintains that the novelist must finally 'leave the company and withdraw, alone, to that mysterious room where his body is hardened and fashioned into permanence by processes which, if they elude the critic, hold for him so profound a fascination' (*E2*, p. 136). Clearly this withdrawal in which the body is hardened and immortalised resembles death. The artist cannot participate in life and maintain an aesthetic distance simultaneously. The traditional association of the small chamber with the grave is drawn more explicitly in *Mrs Dalloway*: having withdrawn to her attic room, Clarissa reflects 'Narrower and narrower would her bed be. The candle was half burnt down' (*MD*, p. 48). The artist, then, must balance the distance and isolation provided by his room with the immediacy and diffusion of the outdoors. If he does not intermittently allow himself to be inspired by life outside, the withdrawal necessary to acquire a perspective becomes a confinement which distorts it.

Virginia Woolf's choice of rooms as symbols of consciousness, identity and isolation may be due to the fact that she was repeatedly impressed by the extent to which they express the individuality of their inhabitants. Her admiration for Sickert's art was due, in part, to 'the intimacy that seems to exist in Sickert's pictures between his people and their rooms. The bed, the chest of drawers, the one picture and the vase on the mantelpiece are all expressive of the owner' (*E2*, p. 239). Often, in her diary, Virginia Woolf described people by sketching their rooms, which she considered the reflection of their way of thinking.[18] She was inspired by the atmosphere of a room because, for her, it represented a distillation of its owner's personality, and therefore provided an immediate and vivid insight into another person's life that would be withheld in a more anonymous setting. Thus, she wrote to Ethel Smyth:

Please if ever I come again, dont meet me . . . but let me find
you among your things – you cant think what a shock of emotion
it gives me – seeing people among their things – I've lots such
scenes in my head; the whole of life presented – the other
persons life – for 10 seconds; and then it goes; and comes again;
so next time dont meet me.   (L5, p. 70)

Although Virginia Woolf found rooms expressive, she realised
that this quality could be deceptive. Jacob's room, for example, is
in many respects misleading and open to various interpretations
(is it a rose or a ram's skull carved in the wood over the doorway?).
Of course, it may be argued that this element of uncertainty is
further evidence of the room's expressiveness: Jacob's appearance
is ambiguous as well. Yet, if we assume that the room bears any
real resemblance to Jacob, we also suspect that we are merely
constructing a comforting fiction. Indeed, it may seem that the
reverse is true: far from leaving our imprint upon a room, it is the
room that determines our way of being. Bernard's remark, 'There
are many rooms – many Bernards' (W, p. 284), may be interpreted
in two ways: different rooms may reflect the different facets of
Bernard's character or, perhaps, Bernard himself refashions his
personality to suit the atmosphere of a new room.

In 'The Lady in the Looking-Glass', Virginia Woolf implies that
it is naïve to believe that a room reflects its owner. The narrator
initially assumes that there is a correspondence between Isabella
and her room:

she was filled with thoughts. Her mind was like her room, in
which lights advanced and retreated . . . and then her whole
being was suffused, like the room again, with a cloud of some
profound knowledge, some unspoken regret, and then she
was full of locked drawers, stuffed with letters, like her cabi-
nets.   (HH, p. 91).

Yet when the narrator finally penetrates the veil 'trembling between
one's eyes and the truth' (HH, p. 87), she discovers that 'Isabella
was perfectly empty' (p. 92). By using the word 'empty', which is
usually applied to rooms, the narrator at once recalls and punctures
the illusion that the room expresses Isabella. Often, the sight of
an empty room has a similar effect. The narrator of *Jacob's Room*
admonishes the reader not to attribute feelings to a room: when

Jacob is seduced by Florinda, she observes that 'the sitting-room neither knew nor cared. The door was shut; and to suppose that wood, when it creaks, transmits anything save that rats are busy and wood dry is childish' (*JR*, p. 148). The descriptions of empty rooms which recur in Virginia Woolf's writings emphasise the autonomy of the room. She focuses upon the events within a room that occur without human intervention, such as rustling curtains and creaking floorboards: 'Listless is the air in an empty room, just swelling the curtain; the flowers in the jar shift. The fibre in the wicker arm-chair creaks, although no one sits there' (*JR*, p. 289–90). A sense of alienation accompanies such visions of 'the thing that exists when we aren't there' (*D3*, p. 114). Like the 'eyeless' house in 'Time Passes', the empty room fails to acknowledge, and thereby create, its perceiver.

Yet so persistent is the belief in a mutual relationship between a room and its inhabitant or perceiver that, at the moment of its denial, it returns with renewed strength. The fact that Isabella is 'empty' makes her closely packed room seem fraudulent. Reciprocally, the perceiver of an empty room seems to become insubstantial himself. James Naremore has remarked that 'in Virginia Woolf's descriptions of empty houses and vast landscapes the narrator becomes merely an airy presence, a sort of ghost'.[19]

In an early typescript of *Pointz Hall* (which was to become *Between the Acts*), Virginia Woolf comments upon the difficulty of defining so ethereal a spirit as the perceiver of an empty room:

> But who observed the dining-room? Who noted the silence, the emptiness? What name is to be given to that which notes that a room is empty? This presence certainly requires a name, for without a name what can exist? And how can silence or emptiness be noted by that which has no existence? . . . . But this spirit, this haunter and joiner, who makes one where there are two, three, six or seven, and preserves what without it would perish, is nameless. Nameless it is, yet partakes of all things named. (*Pointz Hall*, pp. 61–2)

Certainly Virginia Woolf, who maintained that the artist should be anonymous and that unity must be the product of assimilation rather than exclusion, would be attracted to the image of an invisible and unnamed 'haunter and joiner'. Yet there is also an element of mockery in this passage. The perennial philosophical conundrums are too earnestly invoked – how can an unperceived object exist? how can a nameless one? Virginia Woolf believed that perception was a creative act, but she was also well enough acquainted with the common sense philosophy of G. E. Moore to consider the postulation of such a spirit slightly ridiculous. Although this meditation is not included in the final version, it does illuminate another passage from *Between the Acts*:

> the library was empty. . . . The light but variable breeze, foretold by the weather expert, flapped the yellow curtain, tossing light, then shadow. The fire greyed, then glowed, and the tortoiseshell butterfly beat on the lower pane of the window; beat, beat, beat; repeating that if no human being ever came, never, never, never, the books would be mouldy, the fire out and the tortoiseshell butterfly dead on the pane.   (*BA*, p. 23)

In this passage, it is man's self-importance rather than his philosophical naïvety that is exposed. Interpreting the beating of the butterfly's wings as a cry for human attention is, Virginia Woolf implies, as deluded as assuming that the wind blows because the weather expert predicted it. The extent of man's presumption is again illustrated by the description of the empty barn. Virginia Woolf interrupts her account of the ceaseless activity of the animals, insects and birds within the barn three times to state that 'The Barn was empty' (*BA*, pp. 119–21). She is clearly playing on the notion that, in the context of rooms and houses, we have defined 'empty' as 'devoid of human beings'. Mrs Sands, approaching the barn, is oblivious to the industry within: 'Had there been a cat she would have seen it – any cat, a starved cat with a patch of mange on its rump opened the flood gates of her childless heart. But there was no cat. The Barn was empty' (*BA*, pp. 120–1).

In her efforts to correct this presumption, Virginia Woolf stressed the fact that a room will endure despite us. The rooms in her writings are often monuments to the past, while their transitory inhabitants reflect the present moment. Katharine Hilbery's unhealthy preoccupation with the past, for example, is illustrated by her preference for the study, 'a deep pool of past time' which is 'undisturbed by the sounds of the present moment' (*ND*, p. 114). Jacob's room in London is an expression of a style of architecture, not of any of its fleeting owners:

This black wooden box, upon which his name was still legible in white paint, stood beneath the long window of the sitting-room. . . . The rooms are shapely, the ceilings high; over the doorway a rose, or a ram's skull, is carved in the wood. The eighteenth century has its distinction. (*JR*, p. 113).

The faded legibility of Jacob's name on his letter box suggests that the erasure of his identity is in progress even during his occupancy. Previously, Jacob had rooms at college, a familiar emblem of the passing of generations. On his travels, he is just one of a procession of visitors who occupy anonymous hotel and guest rooms.

The temptation to view a room as a vehicle of self-expression must be resisted, then, particularly by writers when they create rooms of fiction. Such projections indicate a lack of respect for the autonomy of other things. They also severely limit the artist's range: the basis of Virginia Woolf's harsh judgement of *Ulysses* in 'Modern Fiction' is the sense that Joyce conveyed to her 'of being in a bright yet narrow room, confined and shut in . . . centred in a self which . . . never embraces or creates what is outside itself and beyond' (*E2*, pp. 107–8). She wanted the rooms of her own fiction to be more inclusive: 'is one pliant & rich enough', she wondered in her diary, 'to provide a wall for the book from oneself without its becoming . . . narrow and restricting?' (*D2*, p. 14).

THRESHOLDS

A threshold frames the scene it encloses in a more direct manner than a room. In Virginia Woolf's writings, characters often hesitate at a threshold and momentarily acquire the unity and consonance of a work of art. A scene at a threshold is invoked in 'Three Pictures' to support the narrator's contention that 'It is impossible that one should not see pictures': 'You see me leaning against the door of the smithy with a horseshoe in my hand and you think as you go by: "How picturesque!"' (*E4*, p. 151).

The blacksmith at the door is picturesque in so far as his attitude suggests a painting. But the secondary meanings of 'picturesque' – charming and quaint – which it is likely the onlooker has in mind are misleading. The narrator observes that such impressions are usually 'quite wrong' (*E4*, p. 151). The frames of life can be deceptive, particularly when they display the scenes they enclose to advantage. In 'Three Pictures', the narrator is himself beguiled by a charming 'picture' of a sailor's homecoming which is, again, framed by a threshold. Later he is unable to reconcile this picture with an anguished cry in the night:

> One saw it all over again producing various little details. . . . So they had stood at the cottage door, he with his bundle on his back, she just lightly touching his sleeve with her hand. . . . Thus gradually going over the picture in every detail, one persuaded oneself by degrees that it was far more likely that this calm and content and goodwill lay beneath the surface than anything treacherous, sinister. (*E4*, p. 151)

The narrator's serenity is short-lived, however, for he learns that the cry in the night was the lament of the sailor's widow. Like many of Virginia Woolf's short stories, 'Three Pictures' is a cautionary tale: life may retaliate if it is subjected to artistic manipulation.[20] Virginia Woolf turned to the frames provided by life to avoid imposing her own designs, but she was aware that such a strategy could result in a refinement of the very error she wished to avert. 'Three Pictures' demonstrates the need to resist the temptation to misuse the frames of life.

If these frames are properly viewed, their effect is not to arrange life but to intensify it. A threshold isolates the scene it encloses. Separated from the accidental conditions of his surroundings, a figure pausing at a threshold becomes vividly realised. The onlooker glimpses a presence which, for the most part, is 'wreathed about with chatter, defaced, obscured' (*MD*, p. 277). It is in this essential aspect that Clarissa appears at the threshold to Peter Walsh, and the effect, it is emphasised, is not picturesque:

> She came into a room; she stood, as he had often seen her, in a doorway with lots of people round her. But it was Clarissa one remembered. Not that she was striking; not beautiful at all, there was nothing picturesque about her; she never said anything specially clever; there she was, however; there she was. (*MD*, p. 116)

Paradoxically, the moment at which a character appears memorably distinct in Virginia Woolf's writings – standing at a threshold –

is also the moment at which he seems irresistibly emblematic. Lily Briscoe, looking at Mr and Mrs Ramsay, perceives that 'the meaning which, for no reason at all, as perhaps they are stepping out of the Tube or ringing a doorbell, descends on people, making them symbolical, making them representative, came upon them' (*TL*, pp. 114–15). Both of the examples that Lily brings to mind take place at a threshold. The 'symbolical' and 'representative' nature of a figure at a threshold is illustrated in 'The Window': Mrs Ramsay, seated with James at the threshold of the French windows, is the image of motherhood for William Bankes and, for her husband, 'the beauty of the world' (*TL*, p. 61). By enhancing both the particularity and the universality of the figure it encloses, the threshold becomes a means of reconciling Virginia Woolf's respect for the thing in itself with her vision of assimilative unity in which 'everything was partly something else' (*O*, p. 290).

A scene at a threshold lends itself to symbolic interpretations not only because it is framed but also because it occurs at a point at which time is suspended. Mrs Ramsay pauses on her way out of the dining room:

> It was necessary now to carry everything a step further. With her foot on the threshold she waited a moment longer in a scene which was vanishing even as she looked, and then, as she moved and took Minta's arm and left the room, it changed, it shaped itself differently; it had become, she knew, giving one last look at it over her shoulder, already the past.
>
> (*TL*, pp. 172–3)

The threshold is clearly the spatial metaphor for the present moment. To pause at a threshold, therefore, is a way of extending the present, an embodiment of Mrs Ramsay's desire to make 'Life stand still here' (*TL*, p. 249). With that 'step further', Mrs Ramsay leaves the past and enters the future. Her backwards glance towards the past is in keeping with the retrospective question which shapes the dinner party for her, 'But what have I done with my life?' (*TL*, p. 129). And, conversely, in *The Waves*, Jinny, crossing the threshold to a party, looks forward towards the future: 'Here are . . . the expectant rooms . . . this is what I have foretold' (*W*, p. 109). In an excised chapter of *The Years*, Eleanor Pargiter goes to a restaurant where revolving doors usher in an endless stream of diners and the swing door to the kitchen is continuously opening and closing.[21] These doors, like many details in *The Years*, are reminders of the heedless and inexorable way in which the past becomes the future.

At the threshold of the dining room, Mrs Ramsay is not only stepping from the past into the future; she is also leaving behind a work of art and entering the flux of life. As was noted in Chapter 1, Virginia Woolf tended to associate art with the past, since both are contained and immutable. Thus, Mrs Ramsay's dinner party becomes a 'scene' which, having 'shaped itself differently', takes its place among the fixtures of the past. Mrs Ramsay glimpses its final metamorphosis at the moment before it solidifies. Although the threshold may merely separate one room from another, it represents a departure from the familiar, unchanging security of the enclosure and an entry into the unknown. Traditionally, a figure at the threshold is in image of expectancy and unrealised potential. Adages relating to opportunity often refer to an open door or a knock at the door. Virginia Woolf was no doubt relying on these associations to suggest the opportunities available to contemporary women when she chose as early titles for *Three Guineas* 'The Open Door', 'Opening the Door' and 'A Tap at the Door' (*D4*, p. 6n).

Virginia Woolf associates the realm beyond the threshold with the sea. Clarissa Dalloway, who celebrates the moment at the threshold, is compared to a diver, roused by potential dangers. She does not fear the immediacy of life and the present moment, nor does she resent the way in which they conceal their boundaries. Instead, she is afraid of the gradual death which attends her loss of the capacity to absorb

> as in the youthful years, the colours, salts, tones of existence, so that she filled the room she entered, and felt often as she stood hesitating one moment on the threshold of her drawing-room, an exquisite suspense, such as might stay a diver before plunging while the sea darkens and brightens beneath him, and the waves which threaten to break, but only gently split their surface, roll and conceal and encrust as they just turn over the weeds with pearl.   (*MD*, p. 47)

In *The Waves*, the difference between Jinny and Rhoda is emphasised by their conflicting reactions to a door that is continually opening at a party. To Jinny, the opening door represents the exhilaration of the here and now: 'The door opens. The door goes on opening. Now I think, next time it opens the whole of my life will be changed. . . . I am a native of this world. Here is my risk, here is my adventure. The door opens' (*W*, pp. 112–13). Rhoda, however, perceives the opening door as a threat to the tenuous order she has imposed: 'Each time the door opens I am interrupted. . . . I am flung far every time the door opens. I am the foam that sweeps and fills the uttermost rims of the rocks with whiteness' (pp. 115–16). The sea, despite its perils for Rhoda, is the realm where Jinny and Clarissa are in their element: a deliberate superficiality ensures that they will, as Rhoda says of Jinny, ride 'like a gull on the wave' (*W*, p. 114).

A threshold is a point at which an end becomes a beginning. Several of Virginia Woolf's novels conclude with characters poised at the doorway. At the end of *Night and Day*, Katharine and Ralph's position at the threshold suggests that they will succeed in reconciling the claims of the enclosure and those of the outside world. One assumes that Clarissa is standing at the doorway at the end of *Mrs Dalloway*, for Peter Walsh suddenly registers her presence, and the final words, 'there she was', were used previously to describe his response to the pause preceding her entry. The threshold is also, according to Virginia Woolf's diary, where Bernard is standing at the end of *The Waves*: 'He will go straight on now, & then stand at the door; & then there will be a last picture of the waves' (*D3*, p. 301). To end a novel at the threshold is to give it, in perhaps a more literal sense than he intended, the kind of 'open-endedness' that Forster advocates in *Aspects of the Novel*.

This open-endedness may be seen as a reflection of the random nature of life which rarely affords the satisfaction of conventional endings. David Lodge interprets what he calls Virginia Woolf's 'non-endings' or 'false endings' as a means of emphasising the arbitrariness of experience: 'Virginia Woolf closes each book [*Mrs Dalloway*, *To the Lighthouse* and *The Waves*] on an affirmative upbeat . . . but the cut-off point is essentially arbitrary, and it is clear that if the text were to continue another down-beat must inevitably follow.'[22] Yet the fact that two of the three novels Lodge mentions end at the threshold suggests that Virginia Woolf was not stressing arbitrariness as much as endurance. She did not merely reject the distortion of endings; she denied their existence. The frames within her works challenge the integrity of the larger frames in which the works themselves are enclosed.

Virginia Woolf denied the finality of death in the same way she did that of the end of her novels; death itself is represented as a threshold in her writings. In a passage omitted from the final version of *The Years*, Eleanor Pargiter reads Captain Rankin's obituary notice and remembers him leaving the drawing-room on his way to bed as if it had been a rehearsal of his death: 'They had been going up to bed. She looked down at the paper again. It must be him, she supposed. For a second she felt a wish to put out her hand and stop him as he opened the drawing-room door.'[23] The image of stepping across a threshold at the moment of death recurs in a letter to Ethel Smyth: 'they burnt 23 candles round a cake, and we each chose one, and mine – a green one – died first, so I shall be the first to leave the room and go out in to what it pleases you to call Heaven' (*L5*, p. 242; see also *D3*, p. 7). To end *The Waves* at the threshold, therefore, is a gesture of defiance like Bernard's cry, challenging not only the finality of the last sentence but of Bernard's death as well.

MIRRORS

The traditional notion that works of art succeed in so far as they provide mirrors of nature is inverted in Virginia Woolf's writings: mirrors are often valued because they approximate works of art. Of all the frames of life, the mirror resembles a work of art most closely, for it not only encloses a scene but also reproduces it. From a Platonic perspective, both the mirror image and the work of art are copies of a copy. In *Between the Acts*, William Dodge takes advantage of the ways in which a mirror corresponds to a work of art: 'Standing by the cupboard in the corner he saw her [Mrs Swithin] reflected in the glass. Cut off from their bodies, their eyes smiled, their bodiless eyes, at their eyes in the glass' (*BA*, p. 87). Unable to express his gratitude to Mrs Swithin directly, he is able to do so obliquely in the looking-glass. Furthermore, the frame of the mirror removes the source of Dodge's shame – his homosexual body – so that his sense of acceptance is unspoilt.

The mirror also approximates a work of art when the person confronting it exercises a certain amount of control over its contents:

he may arrange his features, his position and even his background, using the glass as if it were a canvas for his self-portrait. The mirrors in Virginia Woolf's writing often reveal the extent to which people are their own artistic creations. Clarissa Dalloway, for example, always approaches the mirror 'with the same imperceptible contraction! She pursed her lips when she looked in the glass. It was to give her face point. That was her self – pointed; dartlike; definite' (*MD*, p. 57). Indeed, posing in front of a mirror is so habitual that virtually everyone has experienced the discomfiture of being caught off-guard by their reflection.[24] In *Between the Acts*, the audience resents the assault of the unexpected mirrors: 'But that's cruel. To snap us as we are, before we've had time to assume . . .' (*BA*, p. 214). 'Our parts' is the unspoken conclusion. Only Mrs Manresa accepts the mirrors' challenge and calmly powders her nose: ' "Magnificent!" cried old Bartholomew. Alone she preserved unashamed her identity, and faced without blinking herself' (p. 217). Mirrors cannot disconcert Mrs Manresa; she has internalised her role. (Another indication that Mrs Manresa has mastered one role is that she is among the few characters who are given only one name, and that a slightly fraudulent one, since her marriage to Ralph Manresa is a mockery.) Ironically, one must be a consummate actress to play the part of an uninhibited 'wild child of nature' (p. 52). Sensing that Mrs Manresa's behaviour is a type of performance, Isa is on guard for evidence of hypocrisy. Yet the fact that the mirrors are unable to reveal any discrepancy between her original and her assumed self is evidence of Mrs Manresa's authenticity, as well as of her virtuosity.[25] Rhoda, in *The Waves*, represents the other extreme: her sense of identity is so precarious that she ducks in front of the mirror and insists 'I have no face' (*W*, p. 45).

Virginia Woolf even personified certain mirrors and represented them as striving to attain the formal perfection of art uncontaminated by human reference. In 'Time Passes', the mirror, like Narcissus, falls in love with its own image, just as an artist, seduced by the order he can impose, rejects the confusion of life:

once the looking-glass had held a face; had held a world hollowed out in which a figure turned, a hand flashed, the door opened, in came children rushing and tumbling; and went out again. Now, day after day, light turned, like a flower reflected in water, its clear image on the wall opposite. . . .

So loveliness reigned and stillness, and together made the shape of loveliness itself, a form from which life had parted. (*TL*, pp. 200–1)

Stillness and loveliness are the ornaments of death. The mirror in 'The Lady in the Looking-Glass' also deprives its contents of life. With its doors and windows open, Isabella's drawing-room contains 'the voice of the transient and the perishing . . . coming and going like human breath, while in the looking-glass things had ceased to breathe and lay still in the trance of immortality' (*HH*, p. 87). The fatal consequences of the mirror's imitation of art serve as a warning to the artist. He must ensure that his work does not disdain life, despite its mixed quality: otherwise, it will become merely a monument to itself.

There are, then, instructive similarities between a mirror and a work of art; the differences between them, however, are equally provocative. The mirror may provide a canvas for Clarissa Dalloway's and Mrs Manresa's self-portraits, but it is also capable of acting independently. Often mirrors are represented as the judges, rather than the servants, of the characters they reflect. Virginia Woolf again inverted a familiar notion – that the eyes are mirrors in which the emotions are reflected – and portrayed the mirror itself as an eye. The looking-glass in *The Waves*, for example, holds its contents '*immobile as if everlasting in its eye*' (*W*, p. 227). This may account for Virginia Woolf's preservation of the term 'looking-glass' in her fiction: from the diaries and letters, it seems that 'glass' would have been her natural choice. In 'The Lady in the Looking-Glass', the narrator describes the manner in which the glass looks, just as, in another short story, 'The Searchlight', Virginia Woolf portrays the light undertaking its own search.

The scrutiny of the looking-glass in 'The Lady in the Looking-Glass' is relentless: it tears away the veil of conjecture 'trembling between one's eyes and the truth' (*HH*, p. 87) and exposes 'the hard wall beneath' – 'Isabella was perfectly empty' (*HH*, p. 92). Paradoxically, an optical illusion becomes the arbiter of truth. Yet the tendency to see the mirror as a harsh judge is not surprising: even after the advent of self-consciousness, fantasies persist which are checked by the prosaic reflections in the glass. In Virginia Woolf's writings, mirrors may correct a character's sense of self-sufficiency by reflecting the presence of things beyond human control. When the Dalloways board the *Euphrosyne*, Rachel Vinrace looks at herself in the mirror with the increased self-consciousness that accompanies the arrival of strangers and realises 'that her face was not the face she wanted' (*VO*, p. 41). Isa Oliver, too, is reminded by the three-folded mirror that her appearance does not correspond to her ideal.

Such discrepancies draw attention to the difference between the frames of art and those of life. The frame of a painting mediates between meaning and chance. The objects within it are chosen and arranged, while without they are dispersed and chaotic. The frames of life, in contrast, include some indication of the uncontainable forces outside their perimeters. Virginia Woolf's tendency to portray mirrors as the medium of encounters with chance may have originated in an incident she relates in 'A Sketch of the Past' to account for her reaction to the Talland House looking-glass:

> I dreamt that I was looking in a glass when a horrible face – the face of an animal – suddenly showed over my shoulder. . . . I have always remembered the other face in the glass, whether it was a dream or a fact, and that it frightened me. (*MB*, p. 69)

In *The Voyage Out*, a mirror acts as an antidote to the sense of indomitability that Terence and Rachel share when they are assured of each other's love: 'But it chilled them to see themselves in the glass, for instead of being vast and indivisible they were very small and separate, the size of the glass leaving a large space for the reflection of other things' (*VO*, p. 371). E. M. Forster quoted this passage at length in his essay 'The Early Novels of Virginia Woolf'.[26] He too extended the perspective in his novels to emphasise the vastness of the non-human world, particularly in *A Passage to India*. Adela and Fielding, however, must witness the failure of humanism before they are able to appreciate the inconsequence of their gestures ('dwarfs talking, shaking hands and assuring each other that they stood on the same footing of insight'[27]), whereas, with mirrors, Virginia Woolf was able to portray the shock of the confrontation between a self-absorbed individual and an indifferent universe. Such a confrontation occurs in 'The New Dress', when Mabel Waring, mortified by the dowdiness of her new dress, sees her minute reflection in Clarissa Dalloway's mirror: 'it was amazing to think how much humiliation and agony and self-loathing and effort and passionate ups and downs of feeling were contained in a thing the size of a threepenny bit' (*HH*, p. 54).

When one is exposed to the critical eye of the looking-glass, it is tempting to take the view that outer reflections are not only relatively unimportant but also misleading. Appearances, as the adage warns, deceive. Virginia Woolf seems to support this contention when she portrays the way in which Mrs Ramsay's beauty diverts attention from her inner life. Lily Briscoe remarks that 'Fifty pairs of eyes were not enough to get round that one woman with. . . . Among them, must be one that was stone blind to her beauty' (*TL*, p. 303). Still, Virginia Woolf was not prepared to sever appearance from reality altogether, as a passage from *The Waves* suggests:

> *The looking-glass whitened its pool upon the wall. The real flower on the window-sill was attended by a phantom flower. Yet the phantom was part of the flower, for when a bud broke free the paler flower in the glass opened a bud too.* (*W*, p. 80)

By adhering to a strict definition of reality and rejecting those phantoms, like the mirror image, which attend it, one can overlook important correspondences. Like the clichés in *Between the Acts*, which evolve beyond their surface meaning, reflections provide a key to reality: the danger lies in accepting them as substitutes for it. Despite Isa's dissatisfaction with her appearance, she admits that 'She looked what she was' (*BA*, p. 22).

Although Virginia Woolf did not dismiss the effect of appearance, she was aware that other factors contribute to one's sense of identity. As the titles 'The Lady in the Looking-Glass: a Reflection' and 'Reflections at Sheffield Place' indicate, she made use of the traditional association between the mind's reflections and those of the mirror. She frequently demonstrates that actual mirrors are of less consequence in shaping our identity than the inner mirrors which nurture and sustain our memories and illusions. Bartholomew Oliver, drowsing in the library, sees 'as in a glass, its lustre spotted, himself, a young man helmeted' (*BA*, p. 24). The narrator of 'The Mark on the Wall' defends the elaborate constructions of the imagination and observes:

> As we face each other in omnibuses and underground railways we are looking into the mirror; that accounts for the vagueness,

the gleam of glassiness, in our eyes. And the novelists in future will realize more and more the importance of these reflections. (*HH*, p. 43)

In addition to the reflections of imagination and memory, there are the reflections provided by the objects of the external world. The multiplicity of such reflections in Virginia Woolf's writing can be taken as evidence of an essentially solipsistic view of human nature. Harvena Richter suggests that Virginia Woolf's preference for visual, as opposed to tactile, images arises from the wish to portray 'the object as a mirror-image of the self. Were the tactile sense fused with the visual, the object as mirror would be impossible, for touch validates the existence of a knowable world beyond that of the self.'[28] Yet solipsism is not the only way to see oneself mirrored in the outside world. The self-effacement of mysticism has the same effect. Mrs Ramsay identifies with the lighthouse beam by relinquishing her identity: 'in this mood . . . one could not help attaching oneself to one thing especially of the things one saw. . . . Often she found herself sitting and looking, sitting and looking . . . until she became the thing she looked at – that light for example' (*TL*, pp. 100–1). Sometimes solipsism masquerades as mysticism: the mystic in 'Times Passes' is suspect, particularly since his attraction to water – pacing the beach and stirring the puddle – is reminiscent of Narcissus.

When Virginia Woolf illustrates the way in which works of art serve as mirrors the effect is double-edged. The self-consciousness associated with mirrors is never more apparent than when the novelist portrays 'the looking-glass of fiction' (*E1*, p. 219). Isa's three-folded mirror in *Between the Acts* is the focus of a meditation of the limitations of art. Looking in the mirror, Isa sees her love for Rupert Haines reflected in her eyes. But the mirror also reflects her dressing-table, a representative of the realm of conventions and appearances, which corresponds to 'the other love; love for her husband, the stockbroker –"The father of my children," she added, slipping into the cliché conveniently provided by fiction' (*BA*, pp. 19–20). The third emotion Isa experiences remains un-named: 'But what feeling was it that stirred in her now when above the looking-glass, out of doors, she saw coming across the lawn the perambulator; two nurses; and her little boy George, lagging behind?' (*BA*, p. 20). Outside the looking-glass, her children still inhabit an Edenic world which does not lend itself to words. Despite her efforts, Isa is excluded from it; her tapping on the window is unheeded. In contrast, a cliché will suffice to describe her relationship with Giles, since it is the literary equivalent of the hackneyed roles they play in their marriage. The words 'in love' are far less satisfactory in expressing her feelings for Haines. The fact that they remain in quotation marks throughout her meditation suggests that, for Isa, they are merely words quite remote from her sensation.

Isa's reference to 'the cliché conveniently provided by fiction' prompts Allen McLaurin to remark that 'This kind of self-consciousness means that art begins to "mirror the form of its own activity" (Cassirer's definition of the highest objective truth).'[29] For McLaurin, the primary role of the mirrors within Virginia Woolf's writings is to demonstrate the inadequacy of artistic representation. He notes that the literature with which Isa is familiar can only supply the words for commonplace emotions. Art does not provide the means to express her deeper feelings or to communicate with her children. Later, William Dodge too will turn to a cliché derived from fiction to describe the state of the Olivers' marriage: 'Their relations . . . were as people say in novels "strained"' (*BA*, p. 127).

A similar effect is achieved in 'A Sketch of the Past'. Virginia Woolf tries, ostensibly, to account for the sense of shame she experienced looking in the mirror at Talland House. After several conjectures, however, she admits that 'Though I have done my best to explain why I was ashamed of looking at my own face I have only been able to discover some possible reasons; there may be others; I do not suppose that I have got at the truth' (*MB*, p. 69). The casual tone of 'A Sketch of the Past' belies the deliberateness of its design. In recalling her attitude towards the looking-glass, Virginia Woolf digresses, repeats herself and abandons the pretence of a logical or conclusive argument. Despite this apparent spontaneity, it is not accidental that a looking-glass is the focus of her diverse speculations. The passage concludes with her censure of the inaccuracies that are encouraged by those who presume to write biographies and memoirs. The art of biography provides a distorted reflection of life: even the autobiographer finds the looking-glass fragmentary.

It is, furthermore, not accidental that the Talland House looking-glass, like Isa's three-folded mirror, is used to illustrate the difference between a child's perception and that of an adult. The looking-glass passage is prefaced by Virginia Woolf's observation that, when recalling childhood experiences, she is

> only the container of the feeling of ecstasy, of the feeling of
> rapture. Perhaps this is characteristic of all childhood memories;
> perhaps it accounts for their strength. Later we add to feelings
> much that makes them more complex; and therefore less strong;
> or if not less strong, less isolated, less complete. But instead of
> analysing this, here is an instance of what I mean – my feeling
> about the looking-glass in the hall.   (*MB*, p. 67)

In order to escape the remoteness of analysis, Virginia Woolf turns
to the looking-glass – itself an emblem of the loss of immediacy.
In a mirror the perceiver is perceived; the subject thus objectified
acquires self-consciousness, with its attendant loss of innocence.
The pane of glass imposes a barrier, dividing the self which, in
its prelapsarian state, was indivisible. Language also entails a
consciousness of separation. It too divides in order to identify. The
looking-glass in 'A Sketch of the Past' acts as both an instance and
an emblem of the loss of the direct and entire experiences of
childhood and the substitution of various unsatisfactory labels and
interpretations. Nowhere is the inadequacy of such substitutions
more apparent than in the biographer's attempt to portray a life in
words. As Virginia Woolf observes, 'people write what they call
"lives" of other people; that is, they collect a number of events,
and leave the person to whom it happened unknown' (*MB*, p. 69).
    Although, in 'A Sketch of the Past', Virginia Woolf criticises the
presumptions of biography and autobiography, the memoir itself
succeeds in avoiding the imposition of the writer's arbitrary design.
The explanations Virginia Woolf offers of her attitude toward the
looking-glass are incomplete and even incompatible. The reader
must judge the relative merits of these diverse accounts for himself:
no compelling interpretation is vouchsafed. Similarly, in *Between
the Acts*, there is an implied comparison of the view of art
represented by Isa's three-folded mirror and that represented by
the shards of mirrors that Miss La Trobe turns upon the audience
at the end of the pageant. As McLaurin observes, the latter
illustrates Virginia Woolf's belief that 'In order to articulate reality
it must be broken up in this way'.[30] Virginia Woolf's strategy in
Between the Acts is the same as Miss La Trobe's: Miss La Trobe 'hits
on the idea of reflecting fragments, the form which Virginia Woolf

chose for *Between the Acts* itself, with its mixture of poetry, narrative and drama'.[31]

Virginia Woolf used mirrors to defy the boundaries of art. Some of her novels end with mirrors turned outward. *Orlando*, for example, ends with the present moment, and though a date (1928) is attached, the final section of the novel is primarily concerned with capturing the essence of the present. Subsequent readers see their own experience of the present reflected in the work. The outward mirror is the mirror of satire and social commentary. It strains the limits of the work of art by encouraging the perceiver to recognise the continuity between its contents and his own life. Other of Virginia Woolf's writings are framed by mirrors that face inward. In 'The Lady in the Looking-Glass', this strategy is quite explicit: the story begins and ends with the statement 'People should not leave looking-glasses hanging in their rooms' (*HH*, pp. 86, 92). The first and third sections of *To the Lighthouse* reflect each other less directly.[32] Even so, the effect of this reflection becomes a component of the story, since the characters themselves are conscious of the continuities between the two days portrayed. The inward mirror is the mirror of self-conscious art which incorporates its own interpretations. It too defies the boundaries of art, since the mirror-on-mirror effect produces a theoretically endless series of reflections. While Miss La Trobe's pageant concludes with an outward mirror, *Between the Acts* itself ends with a mirror facing inward, a return to the encroaching darkness of the opening section. The final chapter of *The Years* acts as both an outward and an inward mirror: its title 'Present Day' points outward, yet, according to Virginia Woolf's diary, it represents 'the other side, the submerged side' of the first chapter (*D4*, p. 221).

WINDOWS

Windows may be seen as effecting certain syntheses Virginia Woolf wished to achieve in her writing: their medium is protective yet transparent; the perspective they afford is detached yet comprehensive. They also combine significant features of the other frames of life, sharing the mirror's sheet of glass, the room's creation of an inside and an outside, and the threshold's position as a passage between the two spheres. Since rooms often serve as metaphors for the mind in Virginia Woolf's works, it is not surprising that windows are connected with the eyes, which usually represent metonymically the various ways in which the mind apprehends the external world. Although eyes themselves have a figurative function, windows add a further dimension by representing not the direct means of perception but the circumstances which both enable and restrict that perception.

Conventionally, glass (often in the form of spectacles) is associated with those preconceptions and biases which become imperceptible to their possessors. Virginia Woolf generally used this convention to draw attention to the inescapable, and hence invisible, prejudices arising from one's place in history, both personal and collective. In 'The Moment: Summer's Night', she observes

> If you are young, the future lies upon the present like a piece of glass, making it tremble and quiver. If you are old, the past lies upon the present, like a thick glass, making it waver, distorting it. (*E2*, p. 293)

Notwithstanding the disparities arising from age, the narrator in *Jacob's Room* maintains that there is also a communal pane of glass, an inheritance which accounts for the otherwise inexplicable feeling of 'overpowering sorrow' (*JR*, p. 77) experienced by all who view the Cornish hills: 'All history backs our pane of glass. To escape is vain' (p. 78).[33]

Virginia Woolf would have also been familiar with James's reference to windows in the preface to *The Portrait of a Lady*. There, too, windows are used to extend an ocular metaphor: it is a short step from 'points of view' to the innumerable windows in the house of fiction,[34] but the latter is perhaps a more apt metaphor in an aesthetic context because it represents the medium through which a vision is communicated. That Virginia Woolf appreciated the fitness of the metaphor is evident from her use of the term 'transparency' to refer to an essential quality of a work of art.[35] At times it appears that transparency is valued not for its own sake but for the revelation it affords: in her centenary essay on John Evelyn, Virginia Woolf admits 'Evelyn was no genius. His writing is opaque rather than transparent; we see no depths through it' (*E3*, p. 49). When she criticised Vita Sackville-West's writing for its lack of the 'thing I call central transparency' (*L3*, p. 302), however, she seems to have considered transparency an end in itself rather than a means (see also *L*3, p. 244).

Nevertheless, transparency may seem a paradoxical goal; it suggests that the aim of art is to erase itself. The effort to ensure that one's window is transparent seems misplaced when it is possible to step outside. This view is strengthened on the occasions when Virginia Woolf stresses the barrier erected by a pane of glass. In *Jacob's Room*, the train window marks the boundary between the tourist and the native, the spectator and the participant:

> Jacob, regretting that he did not come of the Latin race, looked out of the window. . . . And there is a lonely hill-top where no one ever comes, and yet it is seen by me who was lately driving down Piccadilly on an omnibus. And what I should like would be to get out among the fields, sit down and hear the grasshoppers, and take up a handful of earth – Italian earth, as this is Italian dust upon my shoes.   (*JR*, p. 221)

Characters who suffer from more exacerbated forms of alienation are also portrayed as condemned to remain behind a pane of glass. In the short story 'Moments of Being', Julia Craye's remark, 'Slater's pins have no points' (*HH*, p. 101), is seen as an attempt 'to break the pane of glass' (p. 102) imposed by her repressed lesbianism. For Septimus Smith, anaesthetised by war, beauty exists 'behind a pane of glass' (*MD*, p. 133). His method of suicide, throwing himself out a window, reinforces Clarissa's intuition that his death was an affirmation, rather than a denial, of the value of life.[36]

The desire to shatter a pane of glass is not confined to those suffering from a sense of exclusion; it is shared by the characters in Virginia Woolf's fiction who reject contemplation in favour of action. Rose Pargiter bypasses the official channels and breaks windows to express her political discontent. Jinny, the celebrant of immediacy in *The Waves*, is also associated with a broken window:

> 'There is Jinny,' said Susan. 'She stands in the door. . . . She seems to centre everything; round her tables, lines of doors, windows, ceilings, ray themselves, like rays round the star in the middle of a smashed window-pane.   (*W*, pp. 130–1)

Susan responds to the challenge implicit in Jinny's presence by re-erecting the protective boundaries of her domestic life: 'I pile my mind with damp grass . . . with the sound of rain on the roof and the gusts of wind that batter at the house in winter and so protect my soul against her' (*W*, p. 131). More generally, the breaking of a pane of glass represents a moment of sympathetic identification. In Virginia Woolf's essay 'I am Christina Rossetti', the title statement acts as a catalyst, releasing Rossetti from the captivity of the past: 'It is as if a fish whose unconscious gyrations we had been watching . . . suddenly dashed at the glass and broke it' (*E4*, p. 56).

Yet, salutary as the effect is in 'I am Christina Rossetti', Virginia Woolf did not always recommend that we destroy those barriers designed to protect our identity and keep others at a distance. The counter-argument is deliberately overstated in 'On Being Ill': 'sympathy we cannot have. Wisest Fate says no. If her children . . . were to take on them that burden too . . . the only attitudes for men and women would be those of horror and despair' (*E4*, p. 195). In order to restrain our empathy, we require screens. Nevertheless, Virginia Woolf viewed "the screen making habit" with ambivalence, as her evaluation of her response to the sight of two girls reveals:

> My instinct at once throws up a screen, which condemns them. . . . But all this is a great mistake. These screens shut me out. Have no screens, for screens are made out of our own integument; & get at the thing itself, which has nothing whatever in common with a screen. The screen making habit, though, is so universal, that probably it preserves our sanity. If we had not this device for shutting people off from our sympathies, we might, perhaps, dissolve utterly. Separateness would be impossible. But the screens are in the excess; not the sympathy.   (*D3*, p. 104)

The artist relies on such barriers despite their drawbacks: like the attic room, they represent the detachment required for artistic creation. Once their necessity is admitted, transparency no longer seems a paradoxical goal. Virginia Woolf was drawn to glass because it established a partition without the opacity of a screen. She advised Mark Gertler, who was 'tortured' by 'the solidity & the shapes of objects', 'for arts sake, to keep sane . . . & put sheets of glass between him & his matter' (*D1*, p. 176). The writer, whose barrier is composed of words, must ensure that they do not obscure 'the thing itself'. Bernard's 'false phrases' (W, p. 323), the comparisons that 'come like the convolvulus itself trembling between one's eyes and the truth' about Isabella (HH, p. 87), the inadequate similes that frustrate Rhoda at the string quartet, all share a deceptive opacity.

Not all screens, however, are the consequence of our distorted view of things in themselves. According to the Platonic conception Virginia Woolf outlines in 'A Sketch of the Past', things are, themselves, screens that obscure the original pattern. And while the phrases in Bernard's notebook only erect a further barrier, successful art reveals that the 'paraphernalia of reality' can become 'the veil through which we see infinity' (E1, p. 346): 'the object which has been so uncompromisingly solid becomes, or should become, luminously transparent' (E1, pp. 346–7). Thus the artist's window may also represent the ability to combine, as glass does, solidity with transparency. When, in *Jacob's Room*, the narrator glimpses (through a window) the 'spiritual shape' of Jacob and his friends, she describes it as 'hard yet ephemeral, as of glass' (JR, p. 71).

The pane of glass is not the only feature of a window that Virginia Woolf considered problematic; the distance that it establishes between the onlooker and the spectacle is alternately regarded as an advantage and a liability in her work. The latter view predominates: when Bernard comments that he has been spared the suffering of his friends 'because it is the panorama of life, seen not from the roof, but from the third-storey window, that delights me, not what one woman says to one man, even if that man is myself' (W, p. 264), the boast reveals an indifference that is culpable, a detachment which finally sickens even Bernard himself. This negative response to the distance that a window represents may have originated in Virginia Woolf's reaction to her mother's death. She was standing at the nursery window when she saw the doctor leave the house and realised that her mother was dead. Despite the casual tone of the references in her diaries and memoirs to the hypocrisy of her grief on that occasion, the fact that she continued to return to it, even towards the end of her life, suggests that she never managed to overcome her sense of guilt. In almost every account of her mother's death, she mentions her position at the window, as if it symbolised her detachment:

This is the 29th anniversary of mothers death. I think it happened early on a Sunday morning, & I looked out of the nursery window & saw old Dr Seton walking away with his hands behind his back, as if to say It is finished. . . . I was 13, & could fill a whole page & more with my impressions of that day . . . how I laughed, for instance, behind the hand which was meant to hide my tears; & through the fingers saw the nurses sobbing. (*D2*, p. 300; see also *D5*, p. 85; *MB*, p. 84)

When, in *The Years*, Mrs Pargiter seems to be dying, Delia similarly fails to respond appropriately. It is telling that Virginia Woolf portrays Delia repeatedly taking refuge in the act of looking out the window. The empty street below and the tossing branches heralding a storm provide a closer reflection of her emotions – indifference to the death and exhilaration at the crisis – than the attitudes of grief, both feigned and genuine, within the room.

For the most part, in Virginia Woolf's writings, a person at the window is portrayed as a spectator of the human drama. The theatrical metaphor is apt: the view from an upper window resembles that from a balcony seat and the onlooker, turning to the window for diversion, is tempted to see the scene below as a spectacle enacted for his own benefit. The figures on the street acquire the unreality of performers: dwarfed by the perspective, they are merely vehicles for their clothes; their activities seem slightly ridiculous. In *Between the Acts*, William Dodge and Mrs Swithin become, through one of the novel's characteristic inversions, the audience of the audience arriving for the pageant:

here old ladies gingerly advanced black legs with silver-buckled shoes; old men striped trousers. Young men in shorts leapt out on one side; girls with skin-coloured legs on the other. There was a purring and a churning of the yellow gravel. The audience was assembling. But they, looking down from the window, were truants, detached. (*BA*, p. 89)

One can hardly censure the truancy of Mrs Swithin and William Dodge – society itself determined their status as outsiders. In *The Years*, however, Virginia Woolf manoeuvres the perspective so that the reader is, unwittingly, guilty of a more serious offence. Observed from the vantage point of two anonymous women at an upper window, a man on the street becomes the object of speculation:

> What would he do next? Was he going to give his horse a feed? But here a tall woman wearing a coat and skirt of grey tweed came round the corner hastily; and the little man turned and touched his cap.
> 'Sorry I'm late,' Eleanor called out, and Duffus touched his cap with the friendly smile that always pleased her.   (*W*, p. 103)

The jar is similar to that created by an unexpected glimpse of ourselves in a mirror; if we identify with any character in *The Years*, it is with Eleanor. Moreover, the consciousness of having wronged Eleanor by treating her as an object of casual interest is not sufficient to absolve us, for we are made uncomfortably aware of the innumerable occasions when we remain, like the two anonymous women, in ignorance. The episode implicates us even further by forcing us to recognise the continuity between the women's curiosity and our own desire for the narrative satisfactions of plot and resolution. In this way, the passage, like 'Three Pictures' and 'An Unwritten Novel', cautions that life must be respected, not distorted by the instruments of art. Later in the novel, Crosby is also seen from a window, and the effect, again, is to draw attention to the culpability of the perceiver. In the chapter '1913', Crosby's devotion to 'Master Martin', which, in the absence of other reminders of her previous life at Abercorn Terrace, becomes the keystone of her sense of identity, is contrasted to Martin's impatience with a servant who seems to demand some recognition apart from her instrumentality. Having pleaded a false engagement, Martin looks out the window and sees Crosby join 'the little figures slinking along the wet pavement' (*Y*, p. 240). The nonentity to which he has condemned her is reinforced by the chapter's concluding sentences: 'He saw the snow falling on her black bonnet as she disappeared. He turned away' (p. 240).

Despite these cautionary scenes, a window also provides the perspective for the promissory vision of dawn with which the novel ends. The satisfaction that Eleanor derives from the sight of a young couple emerging from a taxi and entering a house seems to indicate that this demonstration of continuity corresponds to the idea of 'a pattern: a theme, recurring, like music', which had, earlier in the chapter, given her 'extreme pleasure' (*Y*, p. 398).

Similarly, in *A Room of One's Own*, the view from an upper window of the convergence of a man, a woman and a taxi gratifies the narrator.[37] She too is drawn to musical analogy: the scene is invested with a 'rhythmical order' (*RO*, p. 145). Again, the sight imparts a sense of continuity, since the participants are portrayed as afloat on 'a river, which flowed past, invisibly, round the corner, down the street, and took people and eddied them along' (p. 144). The perspective established by an upper window need not represent a culpable detachment; it can also provide an opportunity to glimpse the pattern behind the cotton wool. If distance divests the scene of detail, it also reveals its outline. Proximity, on the other hand, obscures our vision; the closest relationships are the least easily discerned. As Virginia Woolf remarked in her diary, 'when one is seeing people often & intimately one cannot say very much about it. I don't see Lytton far enough away to have a clear picture of him' (*D2*, p. 158). Still, she recognised that her art was fertilised by her association with other people. It was, therefore, only half-jokingly that she wrote to Margaret Llewelyn Davies 'My idea is to sit at my window and have my friends dotted about the estate. I should like to see you and Beatrice and Sidney . . . and others of a more frivolous variety dissolving and combining in patterns in the distance' (*L2*, p. 384).

In *The Lyrical Novel*, Ralph Freedman maintains that Clarissa Dalloway's view of the woman in the opposite house 'reinforces Mrs Woolf's concept of *window* as a symbolic passage from inner to outer'.[38] Yet the effect of the scene is more complicated than Freedman suggests, since Clarissa not only looks out a window, but also looks in one in order to see the woman who is, herself, looking out a window. The two acts – looking out and looking in – are distinct and, for Virginia Woolf, the distinction was suggestive. In 'How Should One Read a Book?' she differentiates between two ways of reading biographies and memoirs: one resembles looking out a window, the other, looking in. For the former, one must position oneself accordingly:

> Is there not an open window on the right hand of the bookcase? How delightful to stop reading and look out! How stimulating the scene is, in its unconsciousness, its irrelevance, its perpetual movement. . . . The greater part of any library is nothing but the record of such fleeting moments in the lives of men, women, and donkeys. (*E2*, p. 5)

Although Virginia Woolf labels this type of reading 'rubbish-reading', many of its characteristics appealed to her. It is a communal act, demanding the reader's participation and encouraging him to recognise the continuity between his window and the author's. It is also the sort of reading that comes closest to capturing the spirit of life and the present moment – 'its unconsciousness, its irrelevance, its perpetual movement'. In this respect, it represents the antithesis of the response evoked by works like Sidney's *Arcadia*, which urge the reader to 'draw the blinds and shut the door, to muffle the noises of the street and shade the glare and flicker of its lights', in short, 'to escape from the present moment' (*E1*, p. 19). Although rubbish-reading is more easily assimilated into our everyday lives, Virginia Woolf observes that 'we tire of . . . [it] in the long run' (*E2*, p. 6). With its many digressions and incongruities, the picture it evokes becomes too diffuse; no frame contains it. Eventually we resent the fact that the authors have 'disfigured the story that might have been so shapely' (*E2*, p. 6).

The second kind of reading is that undertaken

> to satisfy that curiosity which possesses us sometimes when in the evening we linger in front of a house where the lights are lit and the blinds not yet drawn, and each floor of the house shows us a different section of human life in being. . . . Then we are consumed with curiosity about the lives of these people. (*E2*, p. 3)

Although in 'How Should One Read a Book?' Virginia Woolf considers the way in which biographies and memoirs gratify this desire, elsewhere she suggests that the mysteriousness of other people's lives also provides the impetus for novels, which all 'begin with an old lady in the corner opposite' (*E1*, p. 324). A common stance of the narrator of *Jacob's Room* – waiting outside a window for a glimpse of Jacob – reflects the constraints imposed on any effort to penetrate that mystery.[39] Clarissa Dalloway's view of the old woman, then, is primarily an act of looking in a window rather than looking out; her conclusion, 'here was one room; there another' (*MD*, p. 193), is not an affirmation of her continuity with the outside world but a recognition of the autonomy of another person:

Let her climb upstairs if she wanted to; let her stop; then let her, as Clarissa had often seen her, gain her bedroom, part of her curtains, and disappear again into the background. Somehow one respected that – that old woman looking out the window, quite unconscious that she was being watched. There was something solemn in it . . . the privacy of the soul. (*MD*, p. 191)

Interestingly, one of the reasons that Clarissa is impressed by the necessity to honour this privacy lies in the fact that the woman in the opposite house is looking out of a window. Relinquishing her identity in her contemplation of the outside world, the old woman is exposed and vulnerable; to turn her into an object of speculation would be to exploit her position. The act of looking in a window and seeing someone looking out recurs in *To the Lighthouse*. It is one of the redeeming aspects of Mr Ramsay's character that, despite his need for recognition, he respects the privacy of his wife's solitude: 'He could not interrupt her. He wanted urgently to speak to her now. . . . But he resolved, no. . . . She was aloof from him now' (*TL*, p. 104).

Mr Ramsay's self-restraint is rewarded: Mrs Ramsay, of her own accord, suddenly rises to meet him. Clarissa is granted a second vision of the old woman who, calmly preparing for bed and extinguishing her light, enables her to come to terms with death. In both cases, it is as though the outer and inner worlds, chance and desire, had conspired to effect the necessary realisation. The same impression is created in *Night and Day* when Ralph Denham looks out the window and sees Katharine Hilbery just as he is about to propose to Mary Datchet: 'This sudden apparition had an extraordinary effect upon him. It was as if he had thought of her so intensely that his mind had formed the shape of her. . . . And yet he had not been thinking of her at all' (*ND*, pp. 242–3). On other occasions, the union of the two spheres is accomplished by a breeze through a window.[40] As was noted earlier, the wind's intervention signals the turning-point of Clarissa's party. Similarly, in *Between the Acts*, the moment of intimacy between William Dodge and Mrs Swithin is heralded by a breeze which also seems god-sent:

all the muslin blinds fluttered out, as if some majestic goddess, rising from her throne among her peers, had tossed her amber-coloured raiment, and the other gods, seeing her rise and go, laughed, and their laughter floated her on. (*BA*, p. 89)

Mr Ramsay is not the only character who observes his wife looking out the window; Lily Briscoe, too, has taken advantage of the frame the window provides. As the progress of her painting reveals, the artist has a particular obligation to respect the mystery of other people. Lily's prospect represents the other side of the aesthetic vision, the view from behind the frame, the perceiver perceived.[41] The window, however, does not correspond to the frame of a painting: Mrs Ramsay and her surroundings resist conversion into a compositionally satisfying design. Indeed, it is stressed that Mrs Ramsay exists quite apart from Lily's endeavours; the first reference to the picture is Mrs Ramsay's reflection that she had forgotten about it. This independence is, of course, acutely apparent when Lily returns to her painting after Mrs Ramsay's death. All her efforts to restore Mrs Ramsay fail; her return can only be effected after Lily has realised the impossibility of willing it: 'one got at nothing by soliciting urgently. . . . Let it come, she thought, if it will come' (*TL*, p. 297). As Virginia Woolf wrote to Gerald Brenan, beauty is the product of failure and renunciation. There is, one suspects, an element of satisfaction in her repeated references to the failure of words and the novel's shortcomings. Rather than attempting to adapt her vision to the more structured genres that she professed to envy, she chose instead to incorporate them into the novel, extending its already unwieldy form and blurring its already indistinct outlines.

Virginia Woolf's attraction to random, flexible and crumbling frames suggests that, like the artists she portrays, she trusted to chance, even though such a dependence could be construed as a failure to pursue her own vision. She shared, and even celebrated, Bernard's vulnerability to accidental sights: 'The old woman pauses against the lit windows. A contrast. That I see and Neville does not see. . . . Hence he will reach perfection and I shall fail' (*W*, p. 98). In a diary entry, she describes an effect that she re-creates elsewhere in her writing:

the squares with their regular houses & their leafless trees, & people very clearly outlined filled me with joy . . . when live people, seeming happy produce an effect of beauty, & you dont have it offered as a work of art . . . somehow it affected me as I am affected by reading Shakespeare. No: its life. (*D2*, p. 273)

This passage echoes her philosophy in 'A Sketch of the Past'. In both instances, Shakespeare is invoked and then dismissed; if life is a work of art, it is not due to the efforts of an artist – it is because 'Chance had so arranged it' (*HH*, p. 86). Throughout Virginia Woolf's writings, a figure glimpsed against the outline of a window represents the redemption of long stretches of non-being, the revelation of the accidental pattern behind the cotton wool.

Notes

NOTES TO THE PREFACE

1. Stanley Fish, 'How Ordinary Is Ordinary Language?', *New Literary History*, 5 (1973) 41–54, see p. 52.
2. R. L. Chambers, *The Novels of Virginia Woolf*, p. 7.
3. Allen McLaurin, in *Virginia Woolf: The Echoes Enslaved*, is a notable exception. He remarks that 'the idea of the frame is of some importance in the aesthetics of Roger Fry and Virginia Woolf. It can convert the everyday scene into a rudimentary work of art' (p. 195). While McLaurin is intrigued by Virginia Woolf's more conspicuous use of framing effects and Fry's remarks on the function of frames, he does not examine the subject in detail.
4. See, for example, Jean Alexander, *The Venture of Form in the Novels of Virginia Woolf*, p. 111; Herbert Marder, *Feminism and Art: A Study of Virginia Woolf*, p. 37; Madeline Moore, *The Short Season Between Two Silences: The Mystical and the Political in the Novels of Virginia Woolf*, p. 65.

NOTES TO CHAPTER 1: ART AND LIFE

1. Jonathan Culler has observed that the 'problem of the frame – of the distinction between inside and outside and of the structure of the border – is decisive for aesthetics in general' (*On Deconstruction: Theory and Criticism after Structuralism*, p. 193). The context of Culler's discussion of frames is Jacques Derrida's 'The Parergon' which examines the above-mentioned phenomenon of the disappearing frame.
2. Recent studies of Fry's influence on Virginia Woolf include Allen McLaurin's *Virginia Woolf: The Echoes Enslaved* and Harvena Richter's *Virginia Woolf: The Inward Voyage*. While both authors allow that Virginia Woolf was an original artist in her own right, each pursues some very tenuous connections. The opposite view, advanced by James Hafley, is extreme as well: 'Virginia Woolf was not intellectually in accord with "Bloomsbury" . . . her own dealings with and solutions to the problems discussed there were precisely her own, and not dependent upon the group of which she was socially at the centre'

Notes

113

(*The Glass Roof: Virginia Woolf as Novelist*, p. 5). More qualified assessments of Fry's influence are proposed by Jean Guiguet (*Virginia Woolf and Her Works*, p. 52) and Jane Novak (*The Razor Edge of Balance*, pp. 18–24).

3. As R. T. Chapman observes, in 'The Lady in the Looking-Glass', life is 'caught within the frame, static, metamorphosed into glass. This mirror image is a metaphor for a process of perceiving reality which is, most often, associated with aesthetics. The mirror here performs the function of formalizing the flux of experience into significant patterns, of imposing order upon the ceaselessly changing' [' "The Lady in the Looking Glass": Modes of Perception in a Short Story by Virginia Woolf', *Modern Fiction Studies*, 18 (1972) 331–7, see p. 336].

4. As a result, someone as prosaic as H. A. L. Fisher, whose 'brain . . . attempts only solid things' (*L1*, p. 320), appears, by virtue of his political activity, to be at 'the centre of things; sometimes one may call it reality, again truth, again life' (*D1*, p. 205).

5. Howard Harper notes several of Virginia Woolf's references to shoes and boots (*Between Language and Silence*, p. 271). He is not explicit but it would seem that he considers them to be images of masculinity. The connection is quite plausible and not at all incompatible with the associations suggested above. In Virginia Woolf's fiction, the pursuit of truth without compromise or illusion is usually considered a masculine activity. In this light, Lily's 'excellent' shoes which 'allowed the toes their natural expansion' may be an indication of her androgyny (*TL*, p. 33).

6. Virginia Woolf's portrait of Mrs Hilbery was based on Anne Thackeray Ritchie, who also believed that the Georgians 'hadn't any writers such as they [the Victorians] had' (*D1*, p. 248).

7. Clive Bell, *Art*, p. 72.

8. David Lodge, *The Modes of Modern Writing: Metaphor, Metonymy, and the Typology of Modern Literature*, p. 70.

9. McLaurin, *Virginia Woolf: The Echoes Enslaved*, p. 28.

10. Admittedly these photographs, particularly the ones in *Three Guineas*, serve a parodic and subversive purpose. Yet it is in *Three Guineas* as well that photographs are appealed to as incontrovertible evidence of the horrors of war, powerful enough to unite all human beings against the ravages they depict. Certain metaphors in 'A Sketch of the Past' suggest that the photographic process also attracted her. In the effort to describe an ecstatic moment, she wrote 'I could snapshot what I mean by fancying myself afloat [in an element] which is . . . exposed to some invisible ray' (*MB*, p. 115). (I have retained allusions to the 1976 edition of *Moments of Being*, despite the publication of a new and revised edition in 1985, because the 1976 edition is based on an earlier draft which is more explicit, if less polished, than the final version.)

11. In his elucidation of Fry's aesthetics, McLaurin notes that 'In normal vision we see things, in artistic vision we look at them' (*Virginia Woolf: The Echoes Enslaved*, p. 51). Fry's association of true vision with the imaginative life as opposed to the selective vision of actual life in 'An Essay in Aesthetics' has affinities with the Russian formalists' notion

of art as a means of defamiliarisation. Victor Shklovsky argued that literature required a new language 'directed at seeing, and not at recognition' ('The Resurrection of the Word', p. 47).

12. McLaurin, *Virginia Woolf: The Echoes Enslaved*, p. 196.
13. Ibid., p. 25.
14. Robert Kiely, *Beyond Egotism: The Fiction of James Joyce, Virginia Woolf and D. H. Lawrence*, p. 226.
15. John Maynard Keynes, 'My Early Beliefs', p. 64.
16. E. M. Forster, *Virginia Woolf*, p. 9.
17. Robert A. Watson notes that the opening of the short story provides 'the microcosmic model which the remaining action, the short story's macrocosm, imitates'. He concludes that the story 'diagnoses . . . the interpretive relations that produce art, but, when they become too rarefied and obsessive, also enclose the writer within a world of his own devising' ['"Solid Objects" as Allegory', *Virginia Woolf Miscellany*, 16 (1981) 3–4, see p. 4].
18. See, for example, Alexander, *The Venture of Form*, pp. 110–11; McLaurin, *Virginia Woolf: The Echoes Enslaved*, pp. 121–4; S. P. Rosenbaum, 'The Philosophical Realism of Virginia Woolf', p. 341.
19. Bell, *Art*, p. 73.
20. Ibid., p. 57.
21. Ibid., p. 72.
22. Ibid., p. 59.
23. Quoted in Mitchell Leaska, 'Virginia Woolf, the Pargiters: a Reading of *The Years*', *Bulletin of the New York Public Library*, 80 (1977) no. 2, 172–210, see p. 202.
24. Quentin Bell, *Virginia Woolf: A Biography*, vol. 2, p. 107.
25. E. M. Forster, *The Longest Journey*, pp. 1–2.
26. Rosenbaum, 'The Philosophical Realism of Virginia Woolf', pp. 339–40.
27. Richter, *Virginia Woolf: The Inward Voyage*, p. 78n.
28. Susan Dick has noted that the mystic's vision and Mrs McNab's are contrasted more explicitly in the manuscript of *To the Lighthouse*, and, from the evidence it provides, she concludes that 'Virginia Woolf endorses Mrs McNab's perspective which, though muddled and inarticulate, is truer to the complexity of experience than is the simple and abstract vision of the mystic' ['The Restless Searcher: a Discussion of the Evolution of "Time Passes" in *To the Lighthouse*', *English Studies in Canada*, 5 (1979) 311–29, see p. 322].
29. This phrase, adapted from a line in Arnold's poem 'To a Friend', became something of a Bloomsbury byword. E. M. Forster used it to mark the difference between the Schlegels and the Wilcoxes in *Howards End*. Lytton Strachey wrote to Virginia Woolf 'There are moments . . . when I seem to myself to see life steadily and see it whole, but they're only moments' (*Letters*, p. 19). And, in a letter to Ethel Smyth, Virginia Woolf alludes to the opening line of the poem: 'Who prop in these dull days my mind?' (*L6*, p. 352). (The original is even more ungainly – 'Who prop, thou ask'st, in these bad days, my mind?')
30. G. E. Moore, *Principia Ethica*, p. 222.

31. James Naremore, 'Nature and History in *The Years*', p. 243.

32. B. H. Fussell, 'Woolf's Peculiar Comic World: *Between the Acts*', p. 277.

33. Richter, *Virginia Woolf: The Inward Voyage*, pp. 139–43.

34. See also Jean Wyatt, 'Art and Allusion in *Between the Acts*', *Mosaic*, 11 (1978) no. 4, 91–100, see p. 93.

35. See also Lucio P. Ruotolo, *The Interrupted Moment: A View of Virginia Woolf's Novels*, p. 221.

36. Ibid., p. 116.

37. See *Bulletin of the New York Public Library*, 80 (1977) no. 2, p. 140.

38. Joan Bennett, *Virginia Woolf: Her Art as a Novelist*, p. 38.

39. McLaurin, *Virginia Woolf: The Echoes Enslaved*, p. 55.

40. Bell, *Art*, p. 68.

41. J. K. Johnstone, *The Bloomsbury Group: A Study of E. M. Forster, Lytton Strachey, Virginia Woolf, and their Circle*, p. 143.

42. Lodge, *Modes of Modern Writing*, p. 44.

43. Ian Watt, *The Rise of the Novel: Studies in Defoe, Richardson and Fielding*, p. 14.

44. Bennett, *Virginia Woolf: Her Art as a Novelist*, p. 98.

45. See also Chapman, ' "The Lady in the Looking-Glass" ', p. 337.

46. In notably similar terms, J. K. Johnstone describes the effect achieved in Virginia Woolf's fiction: 'Apparently, Virginia Woolf wished to emphasize, and in a sense to frame, the vivid scenes in her novels by giving an impression of the vast realms of space and time that surround them' (*The Bloomsbury Group*, p. 331).

47. See too Carolyn Williams, 'Virginia Woolf's Rhetoric of Enclosure', *Denver Quarterly*, 18 (1984) 43–61, esp. pp. 48–9.

48. For a more detailed discussion of circles in *The Waves*, see Marilyn Tanger's 'Looking at *The Waves* through the Symbol of the Ring', *Virginia Woolf Quarterly*, 3 (1978) 241–51.

49. The numerous images of emptiness in Virginia Woolf's writings have prompted considerable critical attention. Noteworthy discussions of their function are provided by B. H. Fussell ('Woolf's Peculiar Comic World', p. 273), Maria DiBattista (*Virginia Woolf's Major Novels: The Fables of Anon*, pp. 27–8) and Allen McLaurin (*Virginia Woolf: The Echoes Enslaved*, pp. 89–90).

50. Frank Lentricchia, *After the New Criticism*, p. 35.

NOTES TO CHAPTER 2: TOWARDS A DEFENCE OF THE NOVEL

1. That she does so in a letter to Hugh Walpole may lead one to assume that she is merely dissociating herself from the kind of novelist he represents. Yet Virginia Woolf also wrote to Vita Sackville-West that 'Thinking it over, I see I cannot, never could, never shall write a novel' (*L3*, p. 221). And, in her diary, she remarked 'I doubt that I

shall ever write another novel after O. [*Orlando*]' (*D*3, p. 176).
2. S. P. Rosenbaum, 'An Educated Man's Daughter: Leslie Stephen, Virginia Woolf and the Bloomsbury Group', p. 53.
3. Quentin Bell, *Virginia Woolf: A Biography*, vol. 1, p. 23.
4. Gerald Brenan, 'Bloomsbury in Spain', p. 293.
5. Allen McLaurin, *Virginia Woolf: The Echoes Enslaved*, p. 54.
6. Walter Reed, 'The Problem with a Poetics of the Novel', p. 64.
7. It is in her insistence on the necessity of such a historical perspective that Virginia Woolf differs from E. M. Forster. S. P. Rosenbaum has noted that 'In *A Room of One's Own* she questions not Forster's devaluing of form in fiction but his formalistic rejection of the history of the novel' ('*Aspects of the Novel* and Literary History', p. 79). As Rosenbaum observes, only a belief in historical progress will enable Virginia Woolf to envisage a time when women novelists will enjoy the same advantages as their male counterparts.
8. Allen McLaurin is prominent among the numerous critics who have taken a painterly approach to Virginia Woolf's writings. In *Virginia Woolf: The Echoes Enslaved*, he discusses her use of colour (cf. David Daiches, *Virginia Woolf*, pp. 87–8), space (cf. Harvena Richter, *Virginia Woolf: The Inward Voyage*, pp. 228–31) and significant form (cf. J. K. Johnstone, *The Bloomsbury Group: A Study of E. M. Forster, Lytton Strachey, Virginia Woolf, and their Circle*, pp. 90–1). Like S. P. Rosenbaum ('Virginia Woolf and the Intellectual Origins of Bloomsbury', p. 21), McLaurin maintains that Virginia Woolf made use of Impressionist and, later, Post-Impressionist techniques in her works.
9. McLaurin, *Virginia Woolf: The Echoes Enslaved*, p. 79.
10. Ibid., p. 55.
11. Quoted in ibid., p. 55.
12. Quoted in Quentin Bell, *Virginia Woolf: A Biography*, vol. 1, p. 138.
13. Barbara Hardy, 'An Approach through Narrative', p. 36.
14. Richter, *Virginia Woolf: The Inward Voyage*, p. 69.
15. Richard Rorty, *Philosophy and the Mirror of Nature*, p. 13.
16. Richter, *Virginia Woolf: The Inward Voyage*, pp. 20–1.
17. See also Nora Eisenberg, 'Virginia Woolf's Last Words on Words: *Between the Acts* and "Anon"', p. 257.
18. Quoted in Quentin Bell, *Virginia Woolf: A Biography*, vol. 1, p. 138.
19. Quoted in ibid., vol. 1, p. 138.
20. Jane Marcus, '*The Years* as Greek Drama, Domestic Novel and Götterdämmerung', *Bulletin of the New York Public Library*, 80 (1977) no. 2, 276–301, see p. 293. Marcus also maintains that *Night and Day* is Virginia Woolf's *The Magic Flute* in 'Enchanted Organs, Magic Bells: *Night and Day* as Comic Opera'.
21. Ibid., p. 296.
22. Marcus is to be credited as well for drawing attention to the importance of Virginia Woolf's early article 'Impressions at Bayreuth' (1909).
23. Clive Bell, *Art*, p. 63. It is not surprising that Virginia Woolf was drawn to musical analogies when writing Fry's biography. In a letter to Mrs R. C. Trevelyan, she wrote 'You have found out exactly what I was trying to do when you compare it to a piece of music' (*L*6,

pp. 425–6). In the biography, she commends Fry's ability to establish 'New rhythms' and to break 'the rhythm before it got quite fixed' (*RF*, p. 296).

24. Quentin Bell, *Virginia Woolf: A Biography*, vol. 1, p. 138.
25. E. M. Forster, *Virginia Woolf*, pp. 21–2.
26. E. M. Forster, *Apsects of the Novel*, p. 170.
27. This impression is emphasised by the fact that Rhoda has the same response to Hampton Court: 'Wren's palace, like the quartet played to the dry and stranded people in the stalls, makes an oblong. A square is stood upon the oblong and we say "This is our dwelling-place"' (*W*, pp. 249–50).
28. Quoted in Jonathan Culler, *On Deconstruction: Theory and Criticism after Structuralism*, p. 198.
29. Bell, *Art*, p. 145.
30. Quoted in McLaurin, *Virginia Woolf: The Echoes Enslaved*, p. 208.
31. Ibid.
32. Roger Fry, *Transformations: Critical and Speculative Essays on Art*, p. 6.
33. Bell, *Art*, p. 36.
34. Since Vanessa Bell was the prototype of Katharine Hilbery, Virginia Woolf chose mathematics to be the equivalent of painting, a choice which reveals her early awareness of the painter's model.
35. Bell, *Art*, p. 140.
36. Quoted in Frances Spalding, *Roger Fry: Life and Art*, p. 212.
37. Bell, *Art*, pp. 143–4.
38. See Jan Heinemann, 'The Revolt against Language: a Critical Note on Twentieth-Century Irrationalism with Special Reference to the Aesthetico-philosophical Views of Virginia Woolf and Clive Bell', *Orbis Litterarum*, 32 (1977) 212–28.
39. Like the narrator in 'The String Quartet', E. M. Forster confesses that music leads him to other speculations: '"How like Monet!" I thought when listening to Debussy, and "how like Debussy!" when looking at Monet' (quoted in E. K. Brown, *Rhythm in the Novel*, p. 70). Yet, in this respect too, Forster departs from Virginia Woolf. Generally, he allows the listener his impressionistic response. In fact, he uses elements of Helen's subjective interpretation of Beethoven's Fifth Symphony in *Howard's End* as a motif in the novel as a whole.
40. James Hafley advances a further, theological, interpretation of the imagery in 'The String Quartet': 'The idea of a happy fall from perfection that is death-in-life to imperfection that is potentiality and freedom – this idea is underscored as the speaker greets an applewoman (Eve) beneath the starry night' ('Virginia Woolf's Narrators and the Art of "Life Itself"', p. 30).
41. Both James Hafley (*The Glass Roof: Virginia Woolf as Novelist*, p. 24) and Harvena Richter (*Virginia Woolf: The Inward Voyage*, pp. 22–4) note the relevance of Leslie Stephen's views on the novel to his daughter's work, particularly his observation that the 'novelist is in the border-line between poetry and prose, and novels should be, as it were, prose saturated with poetry' (*Hours in a Library*, vol. 1, p. 29).
42. The same distinction is used in another context – to differentiate

between two types of novelists – in 'Mr Bennett and Mrs Brown': 'In order to complete [the novels of Wells, Bennett and Galsworthy] . . . it seems necessary to do something – to join a society, or, more desperately, to write a cheque. . . . But with the work of other novelists it is different. *Tristram Shandy* or *Pride and Prejudice* is complete in itself; it is self-contained' (*E1*, pp. 326–7).

43. Frank Lentricchia, *After the New Criticism*, p. 137.

44. S. P. Rosenbaum, 'Bloomsbury Letters', *Centrum*, 1 (1981) 113–19, esp. p. 117.

45. This word recurs in Virginia Woolf's writings, often to refer to an irritation. Clarissa Dalloway is 'rasped' by Doris Kilman. But, like Clarissa, who comes to realise that her hatred for Miss Kilman is, in some respects, more satisfying than her regard for her guests, Virginia Woolf preferred the 'rasp' to non-being.

46. In a different context, Philip Toynbee invokes the same scale to emphasise the novel's potential: the novel 'borders on biography and history on one side, epic and dramatic poetry on the other, and it may legitimately swing anywhere between these two extremes' (quoted in Jean Guiguet, *Virginia Woolf and Her Works*, p. 46).

47. Virginia Woolf returned to the works of Emily Brontë and Defoe as paradigms of poetic and realistic writing respectively. She considered Brontë a poet because, 'inspired by some more general conception' (*E1*, p. 189), she created characters and events that express universal, rather than personal, truths. Defoe, on the other hand, provides the standard of realism, not only for fiction, but for facts as well. When Virginia Woolf wrote a preface to a collection of memoirs published by the Working Women's Guild, she observed that 'Mrs Layton's description of a match-box factory in Bethnal Green' possesses 'something of the accuracy and clarity of a description by Defoe' (*E4*, p. 147).

48. T. S. Eliot, *Selected Prose of T. S. Eliot*, p. 141.

49. Daiches, *Virginia Woolf*, p. 36.

50. Ibid.

51. Its aptness is emphasised by Walter Reed's assertion that 'the most basic feature of the novel' is its 'sense of itself as an "outsider"' ('The Problem with a Poetics of the Novel', p. 63).

52. Percy Lubbock, *The Craft of Fiction*, p. 116.

53. Erich Auerbach, *Mimesis*, pp. 525–53.

54. As Barbara Johnson describes Derrida's intention in his essay 'The Purveyors of Truth' (*The Critical Difference: Essays in the Contemporary Rhetoric of Reading*, p. 130).

55. Joan Bennett, *Virginia Woolf: Her Art as a Novelist*, p. 107.

56. Michael Boyd also comments upon Bennett's evaluation: 'The critic would be wrong, however, to assume that this illusion is sacrosanct. Insofar as the interludes serve the rhetorical function of breaking up the reader's immersion in "the story," they provide their own justification in a reflexive text' (*The Reflexive Novel: Fiction as Critique*, pp. 96–7).

57. Roger Fry, *Vision and Design*, p. 30.

58. Robert Kiely, *Beyond Egotism: The Fiction of James Joyce, Virginia Woolf, and D. H. Lawrence*, pp. 174–5.

59. See Robert Scholes, 'The Contributions of Formalism and Structuralism to the Theory of Fiction', p. 116.
60. David Lodge, *The Modes of Modern Writing: Metaphor, Metonymy, and the Typology of Modern Literature*, p. 37.
61. Jonathan Culler, *On Deconstruction: Theory and Criticism after Structuralism*, p. 124.

NOTES TO CHAPTER 3: FRAMES

1. See, for example, Ralph Freedman, *The Lyrical Novel: Studies in Herman Hesse, André Gide and Virginia Woolf*, p. 230; Jean Guiguet, *Virginia Woolf and Her Works*, pp. 416–17; S. P. Rosenbaum, 'The Philosophical Realism of Virginia Woolf', p. 329.
2. It seems to have held a particular attraction for Duncan Grant and Vanessa Bell. Indeed, the preponderance of windows in the latter's paintings has prompted Frances Spalding to speculate that 'this motif . . . had for her more personal significance. It may reflect on her need for domestic security and on the protected position from which, because of her sex and class, she viewed the world' (*Vanessa Bell*, p. 153).
3. Robert Kiely observes that Virginia Woolf's descriptions of Jacob's rooms function in an analogous way: 'By being permitted to see the imposition of design so clearly, we feel free to imagine both the life it delimits and the life that escapes it' (*'Jacob's Room* and *Roger Fry*: Two Studies in Still Life', p. 154).
4. In her discussion of the framing devices in *To the Lighthouse*, Kathryn Kendzora emphasises the negative implications of the window's inability to impose its own design. For Kendzora, such frames simultaneously foster the illusion of order and expose the ceaseless flux of life. In this way, she concludes, they reveal that Mrs Ramsay's 'moment of eternity' is not 'a glimpse of the ultimate order and harmony at the heart of the universe' but 'merely an illusion of unity and harmony, a moment of drama' ('"Life stand still here": the Frame Metaphor in *To the Lighthouse*', *Virginia Woolf Quarterly*, 3 (1978), 252–67, see p. 260).
5. Henry James, *The Ambassadors*, p. 346.
6. Ibid., pp. 348–9.
7. Barbara Hardy, 'An Approach through Narrative', p. 36. See also Marianna Torgovnick, *The Visual Arts, Pictorialism, and the Novel: James, Lawrence and Woolf*, pp. 182–5.
8. James, *The Ambassadors*, p. 350.
9. Kiely, *'Jacob's Room* and *Roger Fry'*, p. 154.
10. Rosenbaum, 'The Philosophical Realism of Virginia Woolf', p. 329. Jane Novak has also remarked upon the dual function of Jacob's room as an image and 'a formal principle, a geometric shape for a series of experiences like separate rooms that are contrasted by their static or

their kinetic representation' (*The Razor Edge of Balance: A Study of Virginia Woolf*, p. 56).

11. E. M. Forster, *Virginia Woolf*, p. 21.
12. The number and prominence of references to light in Virginia Woolf's writings (particularly in *Night and Day*, *Mrs Dalloway* and *To the Lighthouse*) have encouraged critics to explore the various ways in which she adapted its traditional associations with mysticism, civilisation, consciousness, imagination and illusion [see, for example, Marilyn Samuels, 'The Symbolic Functions of the Sun in *Mrs Dalloway*', *Modern Fiction Studies*, 18 (1972) 387–99; Jean Alexander, *The Venture of Form in the Novels of Virginia Woolf*, p. 19; Herbert Marder, *Feminism and Art: A Study of Virginia Woolf*, pp. 133–52].
13. Freedman, *The Lyrical Novel*, pp. 263–4. See also Michael Boyd, *The Reflexive Novel: Fiction as Critique*, p. 98.
14. Samuels, 'The Symbolic Functions of the Sun in *Mrs Dalloway*', p. 388.
15. See Phyllis Rose, *Woman of Letters: A Life of Virginia Woolf*, p. 51; Novak, *The Razor Edge of Balance*, p. 75.
16. Maria DiBattista, *Virginia Woolf's Major Novels: The Fables of Anon*, p. 36. See also Guiguet, *Virginia Woolf and Her Work*, pp. 412–15.
17. DiBattista, *Virginia Woolf's Major Novels*, p. 41.
18. Sometimes Virginia Woolf suggests that the room is particularly expressive of the female spirit. Howard Harper has observed that Virginia Woolf's rooms represent 'a space in consciousness . . . in most cases, a feminine space' (*Between Language and Silence: The Novels of Virginia Woolf*, p. 69). Suzette Henke similarly associates women with rooms in her discussion of the old woman in the house opposite Clarissa Dalloway's: 'The woman seems ageless, an eternal figure of the female spirit sheltered by houses, rooms, distances and solitude' ('*Mrs Dalloway*: the Communion of Saints', in Marcus (ed.) *New Feminist Essays*, 125–47, see esp. pp. 143–4; see also Ruth Gruber, *Virginia Woolf: A Study*, pp. 82–3). These positions are strengthened by the narrator's comment in *A Room of One's Own* that 'one has only to go into any room in any street for the whole of that extremely complex force of femininity to fly in one's face. . . . For women have sat indoors all these millions of years, so that by this time the very walls are permeated by their creative force' (*RO*, p. 131). For the most part, however, Virginia Woolf did not consider rooms the exclusive domain of women (as her interest in Jacob's rooms, among others, indicates).
19. James Naremore, 'The World Without a Self: the Novels of Virginia Woolf', *Novel*, 5 (1971) 122–34, see p. 129.
20. This is quite clearly the moral of 'An Unwritten Novel'. Throughout the short story, the narrator seems culpably arbitrary in deciding such details as whether a centrepiece should be ferns or rhododendrons: the latter which would give the atmosphere a 'fling of red and white' (*HH*, p. 21) are finally rejected on the grounds of improbability. Yet, at the end of the story, the narrator's whimsy is checked by 'Minnie's' refusal to conform to her imaginative construct. In choosing among innumerable possibilities, the narrator had only considered the claims

of art – probability, consistency and pathos, among others. Consequently, she serves as a warning to all artists to respect life rather than convert it into material for art.

21. Quoted in Grace Radin, ' "Two enormous chunks": Episodes Excluded during the Final Revision of *The Years*', *Bulletin of the New York Public Library*, 80 (1977) no. 2, 221–51, see esp. pp. 246–9.
22. David Lodge, *The Modes of Modern Writing: Metaphor, Metonymy, and the Typology of Modern Literature*, p. 180.
23. Quoted in Radin, ' "Two enormous chunks" ', p. 233.
24. Aging sensualists, like Jinny in *The Waves*, are particularly agitated by the experience: 'But look – there is my body in that looking-glass. How solitary, how shrunk, how aged. . . . I stand here, palpitating, trembling. But I will not be afraid. . . . It was only for a moment, catching sight of myself before I had time to prepare myself as I always prepare myself for the sight of myself, that I quailed' (*W*, p. 210).
25. Maria DiBattista also cites this incident as proof that 'Mrs Manresa is one of the most naturally spontaneous characters in the novel essentially because she accepts the necessary artifices of her existence and her social role' (*Virginia Woolf's Major Novels*, p. 222).
26. E. M. Forster, *Abinger Harvest*, p. 121.
27. E. M. Forster, *A Passage to India*, p. 257.
28. Harvena Richter, *Virginia Woolf: The Inward Voyage*, p. 69.
29. Allen McLaurin, *Virginia Woolf: The Echoes Enslaved*, p. 58.
30. Ibid., p. 55.
31. Ibid., p. 56.
32. See Winifred Holtby, *Virginia Woolf: A Critical Memoir*, p. 141.
33. See also Susan Dick, 'The Tunnelling Process: Some Aspects of Virginia Woolf's Use of Memory and the Past', pp. 184–5.
34. Henry James, *The Art of the Novel: Critical Prefaces*, p. 46.
35. Madeline Moore (*The Short Season Between Two Silences: The Mystical and the Political in the Novels of Virginia Woolf*, pp. 224–5, 228), Harvena Richter (*Virginia Woolf: The Inward Voyage*, p. 21) and S. P. Rosenbaum ('The Philosophical Realism of Virginia Woolf', p. 322) have drawn attention to Virginia Woolf's apparent indebtedness to G. E. Moore, who chose the same metaphor to describe the nature of consciousness in 'The Refutation of Idealism' (p. 20). Rosenbaum notes, as well, Virginia Woolf's attraction to the more complex metaphor of translucence to characterise consciousness ('Philosophical Realism', p. 327). In 'A Burning Glass: Reflection in Virginia Woolf', Hermione Lee considers in detail the numerous images which combine glass and light in Virginia Woolf's writing.
36. Ralph Freedman stresses that, although windows foster the illusion of communion with the outside world, they are essentially barriers (*The Lyrical Novel*, p. 231). Jean Guiguet makes a similar observation, although he clearly underestimates Virginia Woolf's self-awareness, when he suggests that she was, 'unconsciously no doubt' (*Virginia Woolf and Her Works*, p. 417), drawn to portray scenes through windows because their frames and their sheets of glass protected her from 'the experience of her senses' which she found 'too violent and

tumultuous', and satisfied her 'obscure need for structure and form' (ibid.). John Graham interprets Septimus's suicide as a way of escaping time and achieving union with the sun, a symbol of divine revelation ['Time in the Novels of Virginia Woolf', *University of Toronto Quarterly*, 18 (1948–9) 186–201, see p. 189]. James Naremore similarly notes that in death Septimus escapes 'the ultimate isolation of the individual ego' and reaches 'the world outside' (*The World Without a Self: Virginia Woolf and the Novel*, p. 243).

37. The correspondence between these two scenes has been noted by James Naremore ('Nature and History in *The Years*', pp. 260–1), Dorothy Brewster (*Virginia Woolf's London*, p. 111) and Nancy Bazin (*Virginia Woolf and the Androgynous Vision*, p. 176), among others.

38. Freedman, *The Lyrical Novel*, p. 225.

39. In fact, the narrator, in describing her position, seems to be outlining the narrative strategy of *Jacob's Room* itself: 'The march that the mind keeps beneath the windows of others is queer enough. Now distracted by brown panelling; now by a fern in a pot; here improvising a few phrases to dance with the barrel-organ . . . yet all the while having for centre, for magnet, a young man alone in his room' (*JR*, p. 154).

40. Virginia Woolf's portrayal of the wind as a beneficent presence may have its origins in her first memory: 'It is of hearing the blind draw its little acorn across the floor as the wind blew the blind out. It is of . . . feeling the purest ecstasy I can conceive' (*MB*, pp. 64–5).

41. Similarly, as Robert Kiely observes, in *Between the Acts*, Miss La Trobe is not only 'director and actor, she is also a spectator. From her hidden vantage point, she observes the audience as though they were performers' (*Beyond Egotism: The Fiction of James Joyce, Virginia Woolf, and D. H. Lawrence*, p. 234).

Bibliography

PRIMARY SOURCES

Woolf, Virginia, '"Anon" and "The Reader": Virginia Woolf's Last Essay', ed. Brenda R. Silver, *Twentieth Century Literature*, 25 (1979) 356–441.

——, *Between the Acts* (1941), Uniform Edition (London: Hogarth Press, 1953).

——, *Books and Portraits: Some Further Selections from the Literary and Biographical Writings of Virginia Woolf*, ed. Mary Lyon (London: Hogarth Press, 1977).

——, *Collected Essays*, ed. Leonard Woolf, 4 vols (London: Hogarth Press, 1966–7).

——, *The Complete Shorter Fiction of Virginia Woolf*, ed. Susan Dick (London: Hogarth Press, 1985).

——, *The Diary of Virginia Woolf*, ed. Anne Olivier Bell, vol. 1: *1915–1919*; vol. 2: *1920–1924*; vol. 3: *1925–1930*; vol. 4: *1931–1935*; vol. 5: *1936–1941* (London: Hogarth Press, 1977–84).

——, *Flush: A Biography* (1933), Uniform Edition (London: Hogarth Press, 1933).

——, *Freshwater, A Comedy*, ed. Lucio P. Ruotolo (New York: Harcourt, 1976).

——, 'Friendship's Gallery', ed. Ellen Hawkes, *Twentieth Century Literature*, 25 (1979) 270–302.

——, *A Haunted House and Other Short Stories* (London: Hogarth Press, 1944).

——, Introduction, *Mrs Dalloway* (New York: Modern Library, Random House, 1928).

——, *Jacob's Room* (1922), Uniform Edition (London: Hogarth Press, 1929).

——, 'Virginia Woolf's *The Journal of Mistress Joan Martyn*', ed. Susan M. Squiers and Louise A. DeSalvo, *Twentieth Century Literature*, 25 (1979) 237–69.

——, *The Letters of Virginia Woolf*, ed. Nigel Nicolson and Joanne Trautmann, vol. 1: *1888–1912 (The Flight of the Mind)*; vol. 2: *1912–1922 (The Question of Things Happening)*; vol. 3: *1923–1928 (A Change of Perspective)*; vol. 4: *1929–1931 (A Reflection of the Other Person)*; vol. 5: *1932–1935 (The Sickle Side of the Moon)*; vol. 6: *1936–1941 (Leave the Letters Till We're Dead)* (London: Hogarth Press, 1975–1980).

——, *Melymbrosia: An Early Version of 'The Voyage Out'*, ed. Louise A. DeSalvo (New York: New York Public Library, 1982).

——, *Moments of Being*, ed. Jeanne Schulkind (London: Chatto and Windus; Sussex University Press, 1976).

——, *Moments of Being*, revised and enlarged edition, ed. Jeanne Schulkind (London: Hogarth Press, 1985).

——, *Mrs Dalloway* (1925), Uniform Edition (London: Hogarth Press, 1929).

——, *Mrs Dalloway's Party: A Short Story Sequence*, ed. Stella McNichol (London: Hogarth Press, 1973).

——, *Night and Day* (1919), Uniform Edition (London: Hogarth Press, 1930).

——, *Orlando: A Biography* (1928), Uniform Edition (London: Hogarth Press, 1933).

——, *The Pargiters: The Novel-Essay Portion of 'The Years'*, ed. Mitchell Leaska (London: Hogarth Press, 1978).

——, 'Pictures', *The Moment and Other Essays* (London: Hogarth Press, 1947) 140–4.

——, *Pointz Hall: The Earlier and Later Typescripts of 'Between the Acts'*, ed. Mitchell Leaska (New York: University Publications, 1983).

——, *Roger Fry: A Biography* (London: Hogarth Press, 1940).

——, *A Room of One's Own* (1929), Uniform Edition (London: Hogarth Press, 1931).

——, *Three Guineas* (1938), Uniform Edition (London: Hogarth Press, 1943).

——, *To the Lighthouse* (1927), Uniform Edition (London: Hogarth Press, 1930).

——, *To the Lighthouse: The Original Holograph Draft*, transcribed and ed. Susan Dick (Toronto: University of Toronto Press, 1982).

——, *The Voyage Out* (1915), Uniform Edition (London: Hogarth Press, 1929).

——, *The Waves* (1931), Uniform Edition (London: Hogarth Press, 1933).

——, *The Waves: The Two Holograph Drafts*, transcribed and ed. J. W. Graham (Toronto: University of Toronto Press, 1976).

——, *The Years* (1937), Uniform Edition (London: Hogarth Press, 1940).

WORKS CONSULTED

Abrams, M. H., *The Mirror and the Lamp: Romantic Theory and the Critical Tradition* (New York: Oxford University Press, 1953).

Alexander, Jean, *The Venture of Form in the Novels of Virginia Woolf* (Port Washington: Kennikat, 1974).

Auerbach, Erich, *Mimesis: The Representation of Reality in Western Literature*, trans. Willard R. Trask (Princeton, N.J.: Princeton University Press, 1953).

Bann, Stephan and John E. Bowlt (eds), *Russian Formalism: A Collection of Articles and Texts in Translation* (Edinburgh: Scottish Academic, 1973).

Bazin, Nancy Topping, *Virginia Woolf and the Androgynous Vision* (New Brunswick, N.J.: Rutgers University Press, 1973).

Bell, Clive, *Art*, new edn 1949 (London: Arrow, 1961).

Bell, Quentin, *Virginia Woolf: A Biography*, 2 vols, 1972 (St Albans: Triad/Paladin-Chatto, Bodley Head and Jonathan Cape, 1976).

Bell, Vanessa, *Notes on Virginia Woolf's Childhood*, ed. Richard A. Schaubeck, Jr (New York: Frank Hallam, 1974).

Bennett, Joan, *Virginia Woolf: Her Art as a Novelist* (Cambridge: Cambridge University Press, 1945).

Blackstone, Bernard, *Virginia Woolf: A Commentary* (London: Hogarth Press, 1949).

Boyd, Michael, *The Reflexive Novel: Fiction as Critique* (Lewisburg: Bucknell University Press, 1983).

Brenan, Gerald, 'Bloomsbury in Spain', in S. P. Rosenbaum (ed.), *The Bloomsbury Group*, pp. 283–95.

Brewster, Dorothy, *Virginia Woolf's London* (New York: New York University Press, 1960).

Brower, Reuben A., 'The Novel as Poem: Virginia Woolf Exploring a Critical Metaphor', in Morton W. Bloomfield (ed.), *The Interpretation of Narrative: Theory and Practice* (Cambridge, Mass.: Harvard University Press, 1970).

Brown, E. K., *Rhythm in the Novel* (Toronto: University of Toronto Press, 1950).

Bulletin of the New York Public Library, ed. David V. Erdman, *Virginia Woolf Special Issue*, 80.2 (1977).

Bywater, William G., Jr, *Clive Bell's Eye* (Detroit, Ill.: Wayne State University Press, 1975).

Chambers, R. L., *The Novels of Virginia Woolf* (Edinburgh: Oliver and Boyd, 1947).

Chapman, R. T., '"The Lady in the Looking-Glass": Modes of Perception in a Short Story by Virginia Woolf', *Modern Fiction Studies*, 18 (1972) 331–7.

Chatman, Seymour, Umberto Eco and Jean-Marie Klinkenberg (eds), *A Semiotic Landscape: Proceedings of the First Congress of the International Association for Semiotic Studies in Milan, June 1974* (The Hague: Mouton, 1979).

Clements, Patricia and Isobel Grundy (eds), *Virginia Woolf: New Critical Essays* (London: Vision, 1983).

Cohn, Ruby, 'Art in *To the Lighthouse*', *Modern Fiction Studies*, 8 (1962) 127–36.

Collins, Judith, *The Omega Workshops* (London: Secker and Warburg, 1984).

Culler, Jonathan, *On Deconstruction: Theory and Criticism after Structuralism* (Ithaca, N.Y.: Cornell University Press, 1982).

Daiches, David, *Virginia Woolf* (Norfolk, Conn.: New Directions, 1942).

Derrida, Jacques, 'The Parergon', trans. Craig Owen, *October*, 9 (1979) 3–40.

DiBattista, Maria, *Virginia Woolf's Major Novels: The Fables of Anon* (New Haven, Conn.: Yale University Press, 1980).

Dick, Susan, 'The Restless Searcher: a Discussion of the Evolution of "Time Passes" in *To the Lighthouse*', *English Studies in Canada*, 5 (1979) 311–29.

——, 'The Tunnelling Process: some Aspects of Virginia Woolf's Use of Memory and the Past', in P. Clements and I. Grundy (eds), *Virginia Woolf: New Critical Essays*, pp. 176–99.

Dowling, David, *Bloomsbury Aesthetics and the Novels of Forster and Woolf* (New York: St Martin's Press, 1985).

Eisenberg, Nora, 'Virginia Woolf's Last Words on Words: *Between the Acts* and "Anon." ', in J. Marcus, *New Feminist Essays on Virginia Woolf*, pp. 253–66.

Eliot, T. S., *Selected Prose of T. S. Eliot*, ed. Frank Kermode (New York: Harcourt, Farrar, 1975).

Fish, Stanley, 'How Ordinary Is Ordinary Language?', *New Literary History*, 5 (1973) 41–54.

Forster, E. M., *Abinger Harvest* (1936; Harmondsworth, Middx.: Penguin, 1967).

——, *Anonymity: An Enquiry* (London: Hogarth Press, 1925).

——, *Aspects of the Novel* (1927; Harmondsworth, Middx.: Penguin, 1962).

——, *Howards End* (1910; Harmondsworth, Middx.: Penguin, 1941).

——, *The Longest Journey* (1922; New York: Vintage–Random House, 1962).

——, *A Passage to India* (1924; Harmondsworth, Middx.: Penguin, 1961).

——, *Virginia Woolf* (Cambridge: Cambridge University Press, 1942).

Franks, Gabriel, 'Virginia Woolf and the Philosophy of G. E. Moore', *Personalist*, 50 (1969) 222–40.

Freedman, Ralph, *The Lyrical Novel: Studies in Hermann Hesse, André Gide and Virginia Woolf* (Princeton, N.J.: Princeton University Press, 1963).

——, (ed.), *Virginia Woolf: Revaluation and Continuity* (Berkeley: University of California Press, 1980).

Fry, Roger, *Transformations: Critical and Speculative Essays on Art* (London: Chatto and Windus, 1926).

——, *Vision and Design* (1920; Harmondsworth, Middx.: Penguin, 1937).

Fussell, B. H., 'Woolf's Peculiar Comic World: *Between the Acts*', in R. Freedman (ed.), *Virginia Woolf: Revaluation and Continuity*, pp. 263–83.

Ginsberg, Elaine K. and Laura Moss Gottlieb (eds), *Virginia Woolf: Centennial Essays* (Troy, N.Y.: Whitston, 1983).

Goldman, Mark, *The Reader's Art: Virginia Woolf as Literary Critic* (The Hague: Mouton, 1976).

Golomb, Harai, 'Different Organizations of Complexity in Music and Literature', in S. Chatman, U. Eco and J.-M. Klinkenberg (eds), *A Semiotic Landscape*, pp. 985–90.

Gordon, Lyndall, *A Writer's Life* (Oxford: Oxford University Press, 1984).

Graham, J. W., 'The "Caricature Value" of Parody and Fantasy in *Orlando*', *University of Toronto Quarterly*, 30 (1961) 345–66.

——, 'A Negative Note on Bergson and Virginia Woolf', *Essays in Criticism*, 6 (1956) 70–4.

——, 'Point of View in *The Waves*: some Services of the Style', *University of Toronto Quarterly*, 39 (1969–70) 193–211.

——, 'Time in the Novels of Virginia Woolf', *University of Toronto Quarterly*, 18 (1948–9) 186–201.

Griffin, Gail B., 'Braving the Mirror: Virginia Woolf as Autobiographer', *Biography*, 4 (1981) 108–18.

Gruber, Ruth, *Virginia Woolf: A Study* (Leipzig: Bernhard Tauchnitz, 1935).

Guiguet, Jean, *Virginia Woolf and Her Works*, trans. Jean Stewart (London: Hogarth Press, 1965).

Hafley, James, *The Glass Roof: Virginia Woolf as Novelist* (New York: Russell and Russell, 1954).
——, 'Virginia Woolf's Narrators and the Art of "Life Itself" ', in R. Freedman (ed.), *Virginia Woolf: Revaluation and Continuity*, pp. 29–43.
Hardy, Barbara, 'An Approach through Narrative', in M. Spilka (ed.), *Virginia Woolf: A Collection of Critical Essays*, pp. 31–40.
Harper, Howard, *Between Language and Silence: The Novels of Virginia Woolf* (Baton Rouge: Louisiana State University Press, 1982).
Harrington, Henry R., 'The Central Line Down the Middle of *To the Lighthouse*', *Contemporary Literature*, 21 (1980) 363–82.
Hartman, Geoffrey H., 'Virginia's Web', *Chicago Review*, 14 (1961) no. 4, 20–32. Also in T. A. Volger, *Twentieth Century Interpretations of 'To the Lighthouse'*, pp. 70–81.
Havard-Williams, Peter and Mary, 'Perceptive Contemplation in the Work of Virginia Woolf', *English Studies*, 35 (1954) 97–116.
Heinemann, Jan, 'The Revolt against Language: a Critical Note on Twentieth Century Irrationalism with Special Reference to the Aesthetico-philosophical Views of Virginia Woolf and Clive Bell', *Orbis Litterarum*, 32 (1977) 212–28.
Henke, Suzette A., 'Mrs Dalloway: the Communion of Saints', in J. Marcus (ed.), *New Feminist Essays on Virginia Woolf*, pp. 125–47.
Herz, Judith Scherer, and Robert K. Martin (eds), *E. M. Forster: Centenary Revaluations* (London: Macmillan, 1982).
Hintikka, Jaako, 'Virginia Woolf and Our Knowledge of the External World', *The Journal of Aesthetics and Art Criticism*, 38 (1979) 5–14.
Holtby, Winifred, *Virginia Woolf: A Critical Memoir* (Chicago: Academy, 1978).
James, Henry, *The Ambassadors* (1903; Harmondsworth, Middx.: Penguin, 1973).
——, *The Art of the Novel: Critical Prefaces* (New York: Scribner's, 1934).
——, *The Wings of the Dove* (1902; Harmondsworth, Middx.: Penguin, 1965).
Johnson, Barbara, *The Critical Difference: Essays in the Contemporary Rhetoric of Reading* (Baltimore, Md: Johns Hopkins University Press, 1980).
Johnstone, J. K., *The Bloomsbury Group: A Study of E. M. Forster, Lytton Strachey, Virginia Woolf, and their Circle* (London: Secker and Warburg, 1954).
Kendzora, Kathryn, ' "Life stand still here": the Frame Metaphor in *To the Lighthouse*', *Virginia Woolf Quarterly*, 3 (1978) 252–67.
Kermode, Frank, *The Sense of an Ending: Studies in the Theory of Fiction* (New York: Oxford University Press, 1967).
Keynes, John Maynard, 'My Early Beliefs', in S. P. Rosenbaum (ed.), *The Bloomsbury Group: A Collection of Memoirs, Commentary and Criticism*, pp. 48–64.
Kiely, Robert, *Beyond Egotism: The Fiction of James Joyce, Virginia Woolf, and D. H. Lawrence* (Cambridge, Mass.: Harvard University Press, 1980).
——, '*Jacob's Room* and *Roger Fry*: Two Studies in Still Life', in R. Kiely (ed.), *Modernism Reconsidered*, pp. 147–66.

——, (ed.), *Modernism Reconsidered*, Harvard English Studies 11 (Cambridge, Mass.: Harvard University Press, 1983).

Kirkpatrick, B. J., *A Bibliography of Virginia Woolf*, 3rd edn (Oxford: Clarendon Press, 1980).

Lathan, Jacqueline E. M. (ed.), *Critics on Virginia Woolf* (Coral Gables, Fla.: University of Miami Press, 1970).

Leaska, Mitchell, 'Virginia Woolf, "The Pargeters": a Reading of *The Years*', *Bulletin of the New York Public Library*, 80 (1977) no. 2, 172–210.

Lee, Hermione, 'A Burning Glass: Reflection in Virginia Woolf', in E. Warner (ed.), *Virginia Woolf: A Centenary Perspective*, pp. 12–27.

Lentricchia, Frank, *After the New Criticism* (Chicago: University of Chicago Press, 1980).

Levine, George, *The Realistic Imagination: English Fiction from Frankenstein to Lady Chatterley* (Chicago: University of Chicago Press, 1981).

Lewis, Thomas S. W. (ed.), *Virginia Woolf: A Collection of Critical Essays* (New York: McGraw-Hill, 1975).

Lodge, David, *The Modes of Modern Writing: Metaphor, Metonymy, and the Typology of Modern Literature* (Ithaca, N.Y.: Cornell University Press, 1977).

Lubbock, Percy, *The Craft of Fiction* (New York: Viking, 1957).

Majumdar, Robin, *Virginia Woolf: An Annotated Bibliography of Criticism 1915–1974* (New York: Garland, 1976).

——, and Allen McLaurin (eds), *Virginia Woolf: The Critical Heritage* (London: Routledge and Kegan Paul, 1975).

Marcus, Jane, 'Enchanted Organs, Magic Bells: *Night and Day* as Comic Opera', in R. Freedman (ed.), *Virginia Woolf: Revaluation and Continuity*, pp. 97–122.

——, (ed.), *New Feminist Essays on Virginia Woolf* (London: Macmillan, 1981).

——, (ed.), *Virginia Woolf: A Feminist Slant* (Lincoln: University of Nebraska Press, 1983).

——, '*The Years* as Greek Drama, Domestic Novel, and Götterdämmerung', *Bulletin of the New York Public Library*, 80 (1977) no. 2, 276–301.

Marder, Herbert, *Feminism and Art: A Study of Virginia Woolf* (Chicago: University of Chicago Press, 1968).

Marin, Louis, 'The Frame of the Painting or the Semiotic Functions of Boundaries in the Representative Process', in S. Chatman, U. Eco and J.-M. Klinkenberg (eds), *A Semiotic Landscape*, pp. 777–82.

Mauron, Charles, *The Nature of Beauty in Art and Literature*, trans. Roger Fry (London: Hogarth Press, 1927).

McLaurin, Allen, *Virginia Woolf: The Echoes Enslaved* (Cambridge: Cambridge University Press, 1973).

Mcisel, Perry, *The Absent Father: Virginia Woolf and Walter Pater* (New Haven, Conn.: Yale University Press, 1980).

Mendez, Charlotte Walker, 'I Need a Little Language', *Virginia Woolf Quarterly*, 1 (1972) 87–105.

Miller, J. Hillis, '*Between the Acts*: Repetition as Extrapolation', in *Fiction and Repetition: Seven English Novels* (Cambridge, Mass.: Harvard University Press, 1982) 203–31.

——, 'Mrs Dalloway: Repetition as the Raising of the Dead', in Fiction and Repetition, 176–202.

Moore, George Edward, 'A Defence of Common Sense', Philosophical Papers (London: Allen; New York: Macmillan, 1959) 32–59.

——, Principia Ethica (1903) (Cambridge: Cambridge University Press, 1959).

——, 'The Refutation of Idealism', in Philosophical Studies (London: Routledge and Kegan Paul, 1922) 1–30.

Moore, Madeline, The Short Season Between Two Silences: The Mystical and the Political in the Novels of Virginia Woolf (Boston, Mass.: Allen, 1984).

Naremore, James, 'Nature and History in The Years', in R. Freedman (ed.), Virginia Woolf: Revaluation and Continuity, pp. 241–62.

——, 'The World Without a Self: the Novels of Virginia Woolf', Novel, 5 (1971) 122–34.

——, The World without a Self: Virginia Woolf and the Novel (New Haven, Conn.: Yale University Press, 1973).

Novak, Jane, The Razor Edge of Balance: A Study of Virginia Woolf (Coral Gables, Fla.: University of Miami Press, 1975).

Pacey, Desmond, 'Virginia Woolf as a Literary Critic', University of Toronto Quarterly, 17 (1947–8) 234–44.

Pater, Walter, Selected Writings of Walter Pater, ed. Harold Bloom (New York: Signet–NAL, 1974).

Pippett, Aileen, The Moth and the Star: A Biography of Virginia Woolf (Boston, Mass.: Little, 1955).

Rachman, Shalom, 'Clarissa's Attic: Virginia Woolf's Mrs Dalloway Reconsidered', Twentieth Century Literature, 18 (1972) 3–18.

Radin, Grace, ' "Two enormous chunks": Episodes Excluded during the Final Revision of The Years', Bulletin of the New York Public Library, 80 (1977) no. 2, 221–51.

Reed, Walter L., 'The Problem with a Poetics of the Novel', in M. Spilka (ed.), Towards a Poetics of Fiction, pp. 62–74.

Rice, Thomas Jackson, Virginia Woolf: A Guide to Research (New York: Garland, 1984).

Richter, Harvena, Virginia Woolf: The Inward Voyage (Princeton, N.J.: Princeton University Press, 1970).

Richter, Peyton E., Perspectives in Aesthetics: Plato to Camus (Indianapolis: Odyssey, 1967).

Roberts, John Hawley, ' "Vision and Design" in Virginia Woolf', PMLA, 61 (1946) 835–47.

Rorty, Richard, Philosophy and the Mirror of Nature (Princeton, N.J.: Princeton University Press, 1979).

Rose, Phyllis, Woman of Letters: A Life of Virginia Woolf (New York: Oxford University Press, 1978).

Rosenbaum, S. P., 'Aspects of the Novel and Literary History', in J. Herz and R. Martin (eds), E. M. Forster: Centenary Revaluations, pp. 55–83.

——, (ed.), The Bloomsbury Group: A Collection of Memoirs, Commentary and Criticism (Toronto: University of Toronto Press, 1975).

——, 'Bloomsbury Letters', Centrum, 1 (1981) 113–19.

——, 'An Educated Man's Daughter: Leslie Stephen, Virginia Woolf and the Bloomsbury Group', in P. Clements and I. Grundy (eds), *Virginia Woolf: New Critical Essays*, pp. 32–56.

——, 'The Philosophical Realism of Virginia Woolf', in S. P. Rosenbaum (ed.), *English Literature and British Philosophy* (Chicago: University of Chicago Press, 1971) 316–56.

——, 'Virginia Woolf and the Intellectual Origins of Bloomsbury', in E. Ginsberg and L. Gottlieb (eds), *Virginia Woolf: Centennial Essays*, pp. 10–26.

Rosenberg, Stuart, 'The Match in the Crocus: Obtrusive Art in Virginia Woolf's *Mrs Dalloway*', *Modern Fiction Studies*, 13 (1967) 211–20.

Ruotolo, Lucio P., *The Interrupted Moment: A View of Virginia Woolf's Novels* (Stanford, Calif.: Stanford University Press, 1986).

Samuels, Marilyn Schauer, 'The Symbolic Functions of the Sun in *Mrs Dalloway*', *Modern Fiction Studies*, 18 (1972) 387–99.

Schaefer, Josephine O'Brien, *The Three-Fold Nature of Reality in the Novels of Virginia Woolf* (London: Mouton, 1965).

Scholes, Robert, 'The Contributions of Formalism and Structuralism to the Theory of Fiction', in M. Spilka (ed.), *Towards a Poetic of Fiction*, pp. 107–24.

Shklovsky, Victor, 'The Resurrection of the Word', trans. Richard Sherwood, in S. Bann and J. Bowlt (eds), *Russian Formalism*, pp. 41–7.

Silver, Brenda R., *Virginia Woolf's Reading Notebooks* (Princeton, N.J.: Princeton University Press, 1983).

Spalding, Frances, *Roger Fry: Life and Art* (Berkeley: University of California Press, 1980).

——, *Vanessa Bell* (London: Weidenfeld and Nicolson, 1983).

Spilka, Mark (ed.), *Towards a Poetics of Fiction* (Bloomington: Indiana University Press, 1977).

Sprague, Claire (ed.), *Virginia Woolf: A Collection of Critical Essays* (Englewood Cliffs, N.J.: Prentice-Hall, 1971).

Stephen, Leslie, *Hours in a Library*, new edn, 4 vols (New York: Putnam's, 1907).

Stewart, Jack F., 'Light in *To the Lighthouse*', *Twentieth Century Literature*, 23 (1977) 377–89.

——, 'Spatial Form and Colour in *The Waves*', *Twentieth Century Literature*, 28 (1982) 86–107.

Strachey, Lytton and Virginia Woolf, *Letters*, ed. Leonard Woolf and James Strachey (London: Hogarth; Chatto and Windus, 1956).

Tanger, Marilyn, 'Looking at *The Waves* through the Symbol of the Ring', *Virginia Woolf Quarterly*, 3 (1978) 241–51.

Torgovnick, Marianna, *The Visual Arts, Pictorialism, and the Novel: James, Lawrence, and Woolf* (Princeton, N.J.: Princeton University Press, 1985).

Toynbee, Philip, 'Virginia Woolf: a Study of Three Experimental Novels', *Horizon*, 14 (1946) no. 83, 290–304.

Vogler, Thomas A. (ed.), *Twentieth-Century Interpretations of 'To the Lighthouse': A Collection of Critical Essays* (Englewood Cliffs, N.J.: Prentice-Hall, 1970).

Warner, Eric (ed.), *Virginia Woolf: A Centenary Perspective* (New York: St Martin's Press, 1984).

Watson, Robert A., ' "Solid Objects" as Allegory', *Virginia Woolf Miscellany*, 16 (1981) 3–4.

Watt, Ian, *The Rise of the Novel: Studies in Defoe, Richardson and Fielding* (1957; Harmondsworth, Middx.: Penguin, 1972).

Webb, Igor, ' "Things in themselves": Virginia Woolf's *The Waves'*, *Modern Fiction Studies*, 17 (1971–2) 570–3.

Williams, Carolyn, 'Virginia Woolf's Rhetoric of Enclosure', *Denver Quarterly*, 18 (1984) 43–61.

Wyatt, Jean, 'Art and Allusion in *Between the Acts'*, *Mosaic*, 11 (1978) no. 4, 91–100.

Zwerdling, Alex, *Virginia Woolf and the Real World* (Berkeley: University of California Press, 1986).

Index

Alexander, Jean, 112 n.4, 114 n.18, 120 n.12
Aristotle, 14, 36
Arnold, Matthew, 25, 114 n.29
Auerbach, Erich, 72
Austen, Jane, 23, 31–2, 49–50

Bazin, Nancy, 122 n.37
Beethoven, Ludwig van, 51, 54
Bell, Angelica, 67
Bell, Clive, 12, 13, 22, 45, 52, 57, 58, 59, 61, 70
 Art, 11, 20–1, 34, 51, 57, 58, 59
Bell, Quentin
 Virginia Woolf: A Biography, 21, 42
Bell, Vanessa, 42, 43, 44, 78, 117 n.34, 119 n.2
Bennett, Arnold, 5–6, 7, 12, 34, 117–18 n.42
Bennett, Joan, 34, 35–6, 72
Benson, Stella, 29
Bizet, Georges
 Carmen, 64
Boyd, Michael, 118 n.56, 120 n.13
Brenan, Gerald, 42, 43, 71, 110
Brett, Dorothy, 49
Brewster, Dorothy, 122 n.37
Brontë, Charlotte, 23
Brontë, Emily, 66, 70, 118 n.47
Browning, Elizabeth Barrett, 65

Cameron, Julia Margaret, 13
Cassirer, Ernst, 98
Chambers, R. L., ix
Chapman, R. T., 113 n.3, 115 n.45
Coleridge, Samuel Taylor, 45
Compton-Burnett, Ivy, 68
Culler, Jonathan, 74, 112 n.1

Daiches, David, 69, 70, 116 n.8
Davies, Margaret Llewelyn, 107
Defoe, Daniel, 66, 67, 70, 118 n.47
De Quincey, Thomas, 47

Derrida, Jacques
 'The Parergon', 112 n.1
 'The Purveyors of Truth', 118 n.54
 'La Vérité en peinture', 56
DiBattista, Maria, 82, 115 n.49, 121 n.25
Dick, Susan, 114 n.28, 121 n.33
Dickinson, Goldsworthy Lowes, 28
Dickinson, Violet, 42

Eisenberg, Nora, 116 n.17
Eliot, George, 67
Eliot, T. S., 35, 44, 62, 68, 69
 Murder in the Cathedral, 68
 'Poetry and Drama', 68, 69
Evelyn, John, 101

Fish, Stanley, ix
Fisher, H. A. L., 113 n.4
Forster, E. M., 15, 25, 51, 55, 56, 79, 116 n.7, 117 n.39
 'Anonymity: An Enquiry', 11
 Aspects of the Novel, 4–5, 48, 55, 65, 91
 'The Early Novels of Virginia Woolf', 95
 Howards End, 25, 114 n.29, 117 n.39
 The Longest Journey, 22
 A Passage to India, 95
 'Virginia Woolf', 15, 79
Freedman, Ralph, 80, 107, 119 n.1, 121 n.36
Fry, Roger, 6, 12, 13, 14, 22, 24, 30, 43, 45, 46, 48, 51, 52, 57–8, 59, 64, 73, 112 n.3, 112–13 n.2
 Transformations: Critical and Speculative Essays: 'Some Questions on Esthetics', 58
 Vision and Design, 12, 27, 48, 72: 'An Essay in Aesthetics', 1–3, 10, 18, 30, 113–14 n.11
Fussell, B. H., 29, 115 n.49